contents

BOW cardigan

SIZES
Sized for Child's 2, 4, 6, 8, 10. Shown in size 4.

MEASUREMENTS
Chest (closed) 26 (28, 30, 32, 34)"/66 (71, 76, 81, 86)cm
Length 13 (15, 17, 19, 20)"/33 (38, 43, 48, 51)cm
Upper arm 11 (12, 12½, 13, 14)"/28 (30.5, 31.5, 33, 35.5)cm

GAUGE
14 sts and 28 rows to 4"/10cm over garter st using size 10 (6mm) needles. *Take time to check your gauge.*

BACK
Cast on 50 (56, 59, 64, 68) sts. Work in garter st, dec 1 st each side every 20th (20th, 24th, 20th, 22nd) row 2 (3, 3, 4, 4) times—46 (50, 53, 56, 60) sts. Work even until piece measures 7½ (9, 10¾, 12½, 13)"/19 (23, 27, 31.5, 33)cm from beg. Place a marker each side of row for beg of armhole. Work even until armhole measures 4½ (5, 5¼, 5½, 6)"/11.5 (12.5, 13.5, 14, 15)cm above markers.

Shape neck
Next row (RS) K17 (18, 19, 20, 22), join a 2nd ball of yarn and bind off center 12 (14, 15, 16, 16) sts, k to end. Working both sides at once, dec 1 st at each neck edge once. Work even until armhole measures 5½ (6, 6¼, 6½, 7)"/14 (15, 16, 16.5, 17.5)cm above markers. Bind off rem 16 (17, 18, 19, 21) sts each side for shoulders.

MATERIALS
Yarn (5)
•14oz/400g, 560yd/510m (14oz/400g, 560yd/510m; 17½oz/500g, 690yd/630m; 21oz/600g, 830yd/760m; 24½oz/700g, 970yd/890m) of any bulky weight wool yarn in pink

Needles
• One pair size 10 (6mm) needles *or size to obtain guage*

Notions
• One separating zipper, 12 (14, 16, 18, 20)"/30 (35, 40, 45, 50)cm from Coats & Clark, F72 Style, #83F mine gold
• Stitch markers
• Sewing needle, thread and straight pins

LEFT FRONT
Cast on 26 (28, 30, 32, 34) sts.
Next row (RS) Knit.
Next row (WS) Sl 1 purlwise (at center front edge), k to end. Cont as established, dec 1 st at side edge (beg of RS rows), every 20th (20th, 24th, 20th, 22nd) row 2 (3, 3, 4, 4) times—24 (25, 27, 28, 30) sts. Work even, placing armhole markers as on back, until armhole measures 3½ (4, 4¼, 4½, 5)"/9 (10, 11, 11.5, 12.5)cm from beg, ending with a RS row.

Shape neck
Next row (WS) Bind off 4 (4, 5, 5, 5) sts (neck edge), k to end. Cont to dec 1 st at neck edge every other row 4 times. Work even until piece measures same as for back.
Bind off rem 16 (17, 18, 19, 21) sts for shoulder.

RIGHT FRONT
Work to correspond to left front, reversing all shaping.

SLEEVES
Cast on 19 (21, 24, 24, 25) sts. Work in garter st for 2"/5cm, then inc 1 st each side on next row, then every 6th row 9 (10, 4, 4, 5) times, every 8th row 0 (0, 5, 6, 6) times—39 (43, 44, 46, 49) sts. Work even until piece measures 11 (12, 12½, 13½, 14½)"/28 (30, 31.5, 34, 37)cm from beg. Bind off all sts.

FINISHING
Sew shoulder seams. With center of bound-off sleeve sts at shoulder seam, sew top of sleeve to front and back between markers. Sew side and sleeve seams.

Collar
With RS facing, pick up and k 42 (46, 50, 52, 52) evenly around neck edge. Slipping the first st purlwise of every row, work in garter st for 1"/2.5cm. Inc 1 st each side on next row, then every other row 3 times more—50 (54, 58, 60, 60) sts. Work even until collar measures 4"/10cm from pick-up row. Bind off, working the first 4 sts as [ssk] twice, before binding off and working the last 4 sts as [k2tog] twice, before binding off (to shape edge of collar). Fold last 3"/7.5cm of collar to RS.

Bow accents (make 4)
Cast on 10 sts. Work in garter st, dec 1 st each side every other row 3 times—4 sts. Inc 1 st each side every other row 6 times—16 sts. Work even until piece measures 3"/7.5cm from beg. Bind off, working the first 4 sts as [ssk] twice, before binding off and working the last 4 sts as [k2tog] twice, before binding off as for collar. Sew bow accents in place on coat front as shown, with "knot" ends at center front. Stitch zipper in place (sewing top end of zipper along collar if necessary). ▌

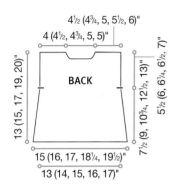

BACK

4½ (4¾, 5, 5½, 6)"

4 (4½, 4¾, 5, 5)"

13 (15, 17, 19, 20)"

5½ (6, 6¼, 6½, 7)"

7½ (9, 10¾, 12½, 13)"

15 (16, 17, 18¼, 19½)"

13 (14, 15, 16, 17)"

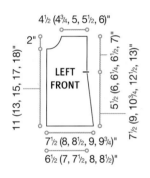

LEFT FRONT

4½ (4¾, 5, 5½, 6)"

2"

11 (13, 15, 17, 18)"

5½ (6, 6¼, 6½, 7)"

7½ (9, 10¾, 12½, 13)"

7½ (8, 8½, 9, 9¾)"

6½ (7, 7½, 8, 8½)"

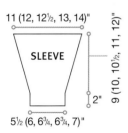

SLEEVE

11 (12, 12½, 13, 14)"

9 (10, 10½, 11, 12)"

2"

5½ (6, 6¾, 6¾, 7)"

Rose Callahan

3

TEXTURED dress

SIZES
Sized for Child's 2, 4, 6, 8, 10. Shown in size 4.

MEASUREMENTS
Chest 20 (22½, 24½, 26, 28)"/51 (57.5, 62, 66, 71)cm
Length 17½ (19½, 23¼, 25¾, 29¼)"/44.5 (49.5, 59, 65.5, 74)cm
Upper arm 7 (8½, 9, 9¾, 10½)"/18 (21.5, 23, 25, 26.5)cm

GAUGES
- 18 sts and 26 rnds to 4"/10cm over St st using smaller needle.
- 17 sts and 23 rnds to 4"/10cm over St st using larger needle.

Take time to check your gauges.

NOTE
Dress is worked in the round in one piece from the top down.

EYELET PATTERN
(over an even number of sts)
Rnd 1 K to end.
Rnd 2 *Yo, k2tog; rep from * to end.
Rnd 3 K to end.
Rnd 4 P to end.
Rep rnds 1–4 for eyelet pat.

BROKEN RIB PATTERN
(over an even number of sts)
Rnd 1 Knit.
Rnd 2 *K1, p1; rep from * to end.
Rep rnds 1 and 2 for rib pat.

YOKE
With smaller needle, cast on 66 (74, 78, 86, 90) sts. Join, and place marker (pm) for beg of rnd, being careful not to twist sts.
Rnd 1 (set-up rnd) P23 (25, 27, 29, 31), place marker (pm), p10 (12, 12, 14, 14), pm, p23 (25, 27, 29, 31), pm, p to end.

MATERIALS
Yarn ④
- 10½oz/300g, 530yd/490m (10½oz/300g, 530yd/490m; 14oz/350g, 610yd/560m; 17½oz/400g, 700yd/590m; 21oz/450g, 790yd/730m) of any worsted weight cotton and acrylic yarn in pink

Needles
- One size 8 (5mm) circular needle, 24"/60cm long *or size to obtain gauge*
- One size 7 (4.5mm) circular needle, 16"/40cm long

Notions
- Stitch holders
- Stitch markers

Rnd 2 [Kfb, k to 1 st before next marker; kfb, sl marker] 4 times—8 sts inc'd.
Rnd 3 Knit.
Rep last 2 rnds 10 (12, 13, 14, 16) times more—154 (178, 190, 206, 226) sts in rnd for body.

Divide for body and sleeves
Next rnd K45 (51, 55, 59, 65), remove marker, place next 32 (38, 40, 44, 48) sts on holder for left sleeve, remove marker, k45 (51, 55, 59, 65), remove marker, place next 32 (38, 40, 44, 48) sts on holder for right sleeve—90 (102, 110, 118, 130) sts.

BODY
Cont in St st (k every rnd), work 6 (6, 10, 10, 14) rnds more.
Next rnd Purl.

Beg pats
Work rnds 1–4 of eyelet pat.
Work rnds 1 and 2 of broken rib pat 5 times. Work rnds 1–4 of eyelet pat once more.
Next rnd Knit.

Shape skirt
Next (inc) rnd Kfb around—180 (204, 220, 236, 260) sts. Change to larger needle. Work in St st until skirt measures 8 (9½, 12, 14¼, 16½)"/20.5 (24, 30.5, 36, 42)cm from inc rnd.

Border
P 1 rnd. Work rnds 1–4 of eyelet pat 3 times. Bind off all sts knitwise.

LEFT SLEEVE
With RS facing, place 32 (38, 40, 44, 48) sts on holder for left sleeve on smaller circular needle. Do not join, but work back and forth in rows.
Row 1 (RS) K to end.
Row 2 (WS) K to end.
Row 3 K1, *k2tog, yo; rep from * to last st, k1.
Rows 4 and 5 P to end. Bind off all sts knitwise.

RIGHT SLEEVE
Work same as for left sleeve.

FINISHING
Sew sleeve seams. ■

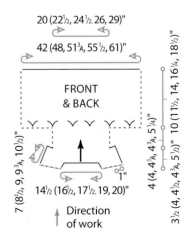

20 (22½, 24½, 26, 29)"

42 (48, 51¾, 55½, 61)"

FRONT & BACK

10 (11½, 14, 16¼, 18½)"

4 (4, 4¾, 4½, 5¼)"

7 (8½, 9, 9¾, 10½)"

14½ (16½, 17½, 19, 20)"

1"

3½ (4, 4½, 4¾, 5½)"

Direction of work

FAIR ISLE
cardigan

SIZES
Sized for Child's 4, 6, 8, 10. Shown in size 6.

MEASUREMENTS
Chest (buttoned) 28 (30, 32, 33½)"/71 (76, 81, 85)cm
Length 15½ (16½, 17½, 18½)"/39.5 (42, 44.5, 47)cm
Upper arm 11 (12, 13, 14)"/28 (30.5, 33, 35.5)cm

GAUGE
22 sts and 29 rows to 4"/10cm over St st using size 5 (3.75mm) needles.
Take time to check your gauge.

SEED STITCH
(over an odd number of sts)
Row 1 (RS) K1, *p1, k1; rep from * to end.
Row 2 K the purl sts and p the knit sts.
Rep row 2 for seed st.

BACK
With MC, cast on 77 (83, 89, 93) sts. Work in seed st for 10 (10, 12, 12) rows. Change to St st (k on RS, p on WS) and work even for 4 rows, end with a WS row.

Beg chart pat
Row 1 (RS) Beg with st 4 (1, 4, 2) and work through st 11, work 12-st rep 5 (5, 6, 6) times, then work through st 32 (35, 32, 34). Cont to foll chart in this way through row 20. With MC only, work even until piece measures 9 (9½, 10, 10½)"/23 (24, 25.5, 26.5)cm from beg, end with a WS row.

Shape armholes
Bind off 8 sts at beg of next 2 rows—61 (67, 73, 77) sts. Work even until armhole measures 5½ (6, 6½, 7)"/14 (15, 16.5, 17.5)cm, end with a WS row.

MATERIALS
Yarn 3
• 10½oz/300g, 830yd/760m (10½oz/300g, 830yd/760m; 14oz/350g, 960yd/880m; 17½oz/400g, 1110yd/1020m) of any DK weight wool yarn in cream (MC)
• 1¾oz/50g, 140yd/130m each in pink (A), hot pink (B), and light pink (C)
Needles
• One pair size 5 (3.75mm) needles *or size to obtain guage*
Notions
• Six ⅝"/16mm buttons

Shape shoulders
Bind off 6 (6, 7, 8) sts at beg of next 2 rows, then 5 (6, 7, 7) sts at beg of next 4 rows. Bind off rem 29 (31, 31, 33) sts for back neck.

LEFT FRONT
With MC, cast on 32 (35, 38, 40) sts.
Next row (RS) *K1, p1; rep from *, end k 0 (1, 0, 0). Beg with row 2, cont in seed st for 9 (9, 11, 11) rows more. Cont in St st and work even for 4 rows, end with a WS row.

Beg chart pat
Row 1 (RS) Beg with st 4 (1, 4, 2) and work through st 11, work 12-st rep 1 (1, 2, 2) times, then work through st 35 (35, 29, 29). Cont to foll chart in this way through row 20. With MC only, work even until piece measures same length as back to underarm, end with a WS row.

Shape armholes
Bind off 8 sts at beg of next row—24 (27, 30, 32) sts. Work even until armhole measures 3½ (4, 4½, 5)"/9 (10, 11.5, 12.5)cm, end with a RS row.

Shape neck
Next row (WS) Bind off 3 (4, 4, 5) sts, work to end. Dec 1 st from neck edge on next row, then every other row 4 times more—16 (18, 21, 22) sts. Work even until piece measures same length as back to shoulder, end with a WS row.

Shape shoulder
At armhole edge, bind off 6 (6, 7, 8) sts once, then 5 (6, 7, 7) sts twice.

RIGHT FRONT
With MC, cast on 32 (35, 38, 40) sts.
Next row (RS) *K1, p1; rep from *, end k 0 (1, 0, 0). Beg with row 2, cont in seed st for 9 (9, 11, 11) rows more. Cont in St st and work even for 4 rows, end with a WS row.

Beg chart pat
Row 1 (RS) Beg with st 1 (1, 7, 7) and work through st 11, work 12-st rep 1 (1, 2, 2) times, then work through st 32 (35, 32, 34). Cont to foll chart in this way through row 20. Cont to work as for left front, reversing all shaping.

SLEEVES
With A, cast on 43 (43, 45, 47) sts. Work in seed st for 1 row. Change to MC and cont in seed st for 9 (9, 11, 11) rows. Cont in St st and work even for 2 rows. Inc 1 st each side on next row, then every 6th row 1 (5, 10, 14) times more, then every 8th row 7 (5, 2, 0) times—61 (65, 71, 77) sts. Work even until piece measures 10 (11, 12, 13)"/25.5 (28, 30.5, 33)cm from beg, end with a WS row. Mark beg and end of last row for beg of cap. Work even for 1½"/4cm, end with a WS row. Bind off.

FINISHING
Block pieces to measurements. Sew shoulder seams.

FAIR ISLE cardigan

Buttonband

With RS facing and MC, pick up and k 69 (75, 79, 85) sts evenly spaced along left front edge. Work in seed st for 13 rows. Bind off loosely in seed st. Place markers for 6 buttons along buttonband, with the first 1"/2.5cm from lower edge, the last ½"/1.3cm below neck edge and the others evenly spaced between.

Buttonhole band

With RS facing and MC, pick up and k 69 (75, 79, 85) sts evenly spaced along right front edge. Work in seed st for 5 rows. **Next (buttonhole) row (RS)** *Work in seed st to marker, bind off next 2 sts; rep from * 5 times more, work in seed st to end.

Next row Work in seed st, casting on 2 sts over bound-off sts. Cont in seed st for 6 rows more. Bind off loosely in seed st.

Collar

With RS facing and MC, beg ½"/1.3cm from right front edge, pick up and k 65 (69, 69, 73) sts evenly spaced along neck edge, ending ½"/1.5cm from left front edge. Work in seed st for 3 (3, 3½, 3½)"/7.5 (7.5, 9, 9)cm. Bind off loosely in seed st. Set sleeves into armholes, sewing top 1½"/4cm to bound-off sts of armhole shaping. Sew side and sleeve seams. Sew on buttons. ■

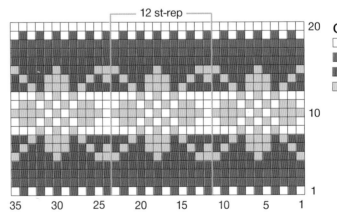

12 st-rep

20

10

1

35   30   25   20   15   10   5   1

COLOR KEY
☐ Cream (MC)
■ Pink (A)
■ Hot Pink (B)
■ Light Pink (C)

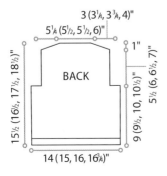

3 (3¼, 3¾, 4)"
5¼ (5½, 5½, 6)"
1"
BACK
15½ (16½, 17½, 18½)"
9 (9½, 10, 10½)"
5½ (6, 6½, 7)"
14 (15, 16, 16¾)"

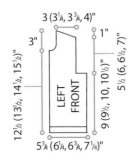

3 (3¼, 3¾, 4)"
3"
1"
LEFT FRONT
12½ (13½, 14½, 15½)"
9 (9½, 10, 10½)"
5½ (6, 6½, 7)"
5¾ (6¼, 6¾, 7¼)"

11 (12, 13, 14)"
1½"
SLEEVE
10 (11, 12, 13)"
7¾ (7¾, 8, 8½)"

RUFFLED dress

SIZES
Sized for Child 2, 4, 6, 8, 10. Shown in size 4.

MEASUREMENTS
Chest 22 (24, 26, 28, 30)"/56 (61, 66, 71, 76)cm
Length 19 (21, 23, 25, 28)"/48.5 (53.5, 58.5, 63, 71)cm

GAUGE
21 sts and 26 rows to 4"/10cm over St st using size 7 (4.5mm) needles.
Take time to check your gauge.

3-NEEDLE JOINING TECHNIQUE
With RS of ruffles facing and the needles parallel, insert a third needle into the first st on each needle and knit the two stitches together; rep until all stitches have been joined.

NOTE
Body is made in one piece to underarms.

BODY
First ruffle
With size 7 (4.5mm) circular needle and MC, cast on 232 (252, 272, 296, 316) sts. Join, and place marker (pm) for beg of rnd, being careful not to twist sts. K 1 rnd. P 1 rnd. Work in St st (k every rnd) until piece measures 2½"/6.5cm from beg.
Next (dec) rnd *K2tog; rep from * to end of rnd—116 (126, 136, 148, 158) sts. Work in St st for 2¼"/6cm more. Break yarn and leave sts on holder.

Second ruffle
With size 7 (4.5mm) circular needle and A, cast on 232 (252, 272, 296, 316) sts. Place marker and join, being careful not

to twist sts. K 1 row. P 1 row. Work in St st (knit every rnd) until piece measures 2½"/6.5cm from beg.
Next (dec) rnd *K2tog; rep from * to end of rnd—116 (126, 136, 148, 158) sts.
Next (joining) row With first ruffle behind second ruffle, join ruffles together using 3-needle joining technique. Work in St st for 2¼"/6cm more. Break yarn and leave sts on holder.

Third ruffle
With size 7 (4.5mm) circular needle and MC, cast on 232 (252, 272, 296, 316) sts. Place marker and join, being careful not to twist sts. K 1 row. P 1 row. Cont in St st (knit every rnd) until piece measures 2½"/6.5cm from beg.

MATERIALS
Yarn (3)
- 7oz/200g, 440yd/410m (7oz/200g, 440yd/410m; 8¾oz/250g, 540yd/500m; 8¾oz/250g, 540yd/500m; 10½oz/300g, 650yd/600m) of any DK weight wool yarn in light blue (MC)
- 3½oz/100g, 220yd/210m (3½oz/100g, 220yd/210m; 3½oz/100g, 220yd/210m; 3½oz/100g, 220yd/210m; 5¼oz/150g, 330yd/310m) in white (A)

Needles
- One size 7 (4.5mm) circular needle, 24"/60cm long *or size to obtain guage*
- One pair size 7 (4.5mm) needles
- One size 6 (4mm) circular needle, 16"/40cm long

Notions
- One size F/5 (3.75mm) crochet hook
- Stitch holders
- Stitch markers
- One ½"/12mm button

Next (dec) rnd *K2tog; rep from * to end of rnd—116 (126, 136, 148, 158) sts.
Next (joining) row With second ruffle behind third ruffle, join ruffles together using 3-needle joining technique. Cont in St st until piece measures 14 (16, 17½, 19, 21½)"/35.5 (40.5, 44.5, 48, 54.5)cm from beg.

Divide for front and back
Next rnd Bind off 12 (14, 14, 16, 18) sts, k46 (49, 54, 58, 61), place sts on holder for front, bind off next 12 (14, 14, 16, 18) sts, k rem 46 (49, 54, 58, 61) sts for back.

BACK
Change to straight needles.
Next row (WS) P to end of row.

RUFFLED dress

Shape armhole

Dec 1 st each side of every RS row 5 (6, 6, 7, 7) times—36 (37, 42, 44, 47) sts. Work even until armhole measures 4½ (4½, 5, 5, 5½)"/11.5 (11.5, 13, 13, 14)cm, end with a WS row.

Shape neck

Next row (RS) K12 (12, 14, 14, 15) and place these sts on holder, bind off center 12 (13, 14, 16, 17) sts, k to end. On these sts only, dec 1 st at neck edge every RS row twice—10 (10, 12, 12, 13) sts. Work even until armhole measures 5 (5, 5½, 6, 6½)"/13 (13, 14, 15, 16.5)cm, end with a WS row. Bind off rem sts for shoulder. With WS facing, rejoin yarn to sts on holder. Dec 1 st at neck edge every RS row twice—10 (10, 12, 12, 13) sts. Work even until armhole measures 6 (6, 6½, 7, 7½)"/15 (15, 16.5, 18, 19)cm, end with a WS row. Place marker at armhole edge, 1"/2.5cm down from shoulder edge.

FRONT

Place 46 (49, 54, 58, 61) sts from front holder on straight needle ready for a WS row.

Work as for back until armhole measures 2½ (2½, 2½, 3, 3½)"/6.5 (6.5, 6.5, 7.5, 9)cm, end with a WS row.

Shape neck

Next row (RS) K12 (12, 14, 14, 15), join a 2nd ball of yarn and bind off center 12 (13, 14, 16, 17) sts, k to end. Working both sides at once, dec 1 st from each neck edge every row twice—10 (10, 12, 12, 13) sts rem each side for shoulder. Work even until armhole measures 5 (5, 5½, 6, 6½)"/13 (13, 14, 15, 16.5)cm, end with a WS row. Bind off rem sts each side for shoulder.

FINISHING

Sew left shoulder seam.

Neck edging

With right side facing, size 6 (4mm) circular needle and A, pick up and k 60 (60, 66, 72, 78) sts evenly around neck edge. Bind off knitwise.
Place right front shoulder over right back shoulder extension, matching bound-off edge to marker. Baste edges together for button loop extension.

Button loop

With crochet hook and MC, ch 6. Fasten off. Sew ends of loop along bound-off edge of right front shoulder, starting at neck edge.

Armhole edging

With right side facing, size 6 (4mm) circular needle and A, pick up and k 60 (60, 66, 72, 78) sts evenly around armhole opening, working through both thicknesses on right armhole at shoulder. Join and bind off purlwise.
Sew button to right back shoulder opposite button loop.

Rosette

With size 6 (4mm) circular needle and A, cast on 10 sts. Do not join, but work back and forth in rows.
Row 1 (RS) Knit.
Row 2 and all WS rows Purl.
Row 3 Inc 1 st into each st across—20 sts.
Row 5 Inc 1 st into each st across—40 sts.
Row 7 Inc 1 st into each st across—80 sts.
Row 8 Purl.
Bind off all sts purlwise. Roll ruffle edge from outside and sew along cast-on edge to form a rose.
With crochet hook and MC doubled, ch 4, join with a slip st to first ch. Fasten off. Thread ends through center of rosette and secure. Sew rosette to center front, approx 1"/2.5cm down from neck edge. ■

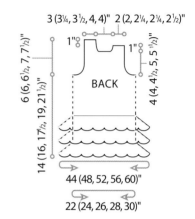

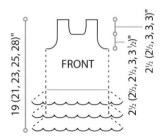

CHEVRON scarf

MEASUREMENTS

Length 43½"/110.5cm
Width at center 5½"/14cm
Width at ends 10"/25.5cm

GAUGE

20 sts and 27 rows to 4"/10cm over St st using size 4 (3.5mm) needles.
Take time to check your gauge.

STITCH GLOSSARY

Kfb Inc 1 st by knitting into the front and back of same st.
Pbkf Inc 1 st by purling in back loop, then knitting in front loop of same st.
M1 Insert LH needle under strand between st just worked and next st. Knit this strand, do NOT twist.
SK2P Sl 1, k2tog, pass sl st over k2tog.

NOTES

1 Scarf is reversible.
2 Incs and decs are worked on both RS and WS throughout.
3 RS and WS reverse at beg of chart 2.

SCARF

Cast on 55 sts. K 2 rows.
Row 1 (WS) K5, [p5, k5] 5 times.
Row 2 (RS) K10, p5, [k5, p5] 3 times, k10.
Place marker on last row worked for RS of scarf.
Rep last 2 rows once, then row 1 once.

Beg chart 1

Work rows 1–46 of chart 1—29 sts.
Next row (RS) K10, p9, k10.
Next row K5, p5, k9, p5, k5.

Rep last 2 rows until piece measures 35"/89cm from beg, end with a RS row. Change marker to mark next row as a RS row.

Beg chart 2

Work rows 1–47 of chart 2—55 sts.
Next row (WS) K10, [p5, k5] 3 times, p5, k10.
Next row [K5, p5] 5 times, k5.
Rep last 2 rows once more.
Knit 2 rows. Bind off. ∎

CHART 1
end with 29 sts

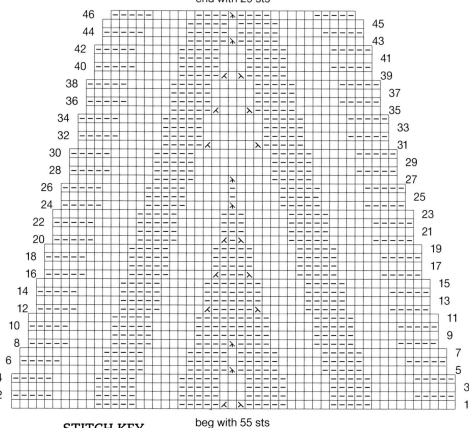

beg with 55 sts

STITCH KEY

☐ k on RS, p on WS
⊟ p on RS, k on WS

☒ k2tog   ☒ SK2P   ℙ pbkf
☒ SKP   Ⓜ M1   ℙ kfb

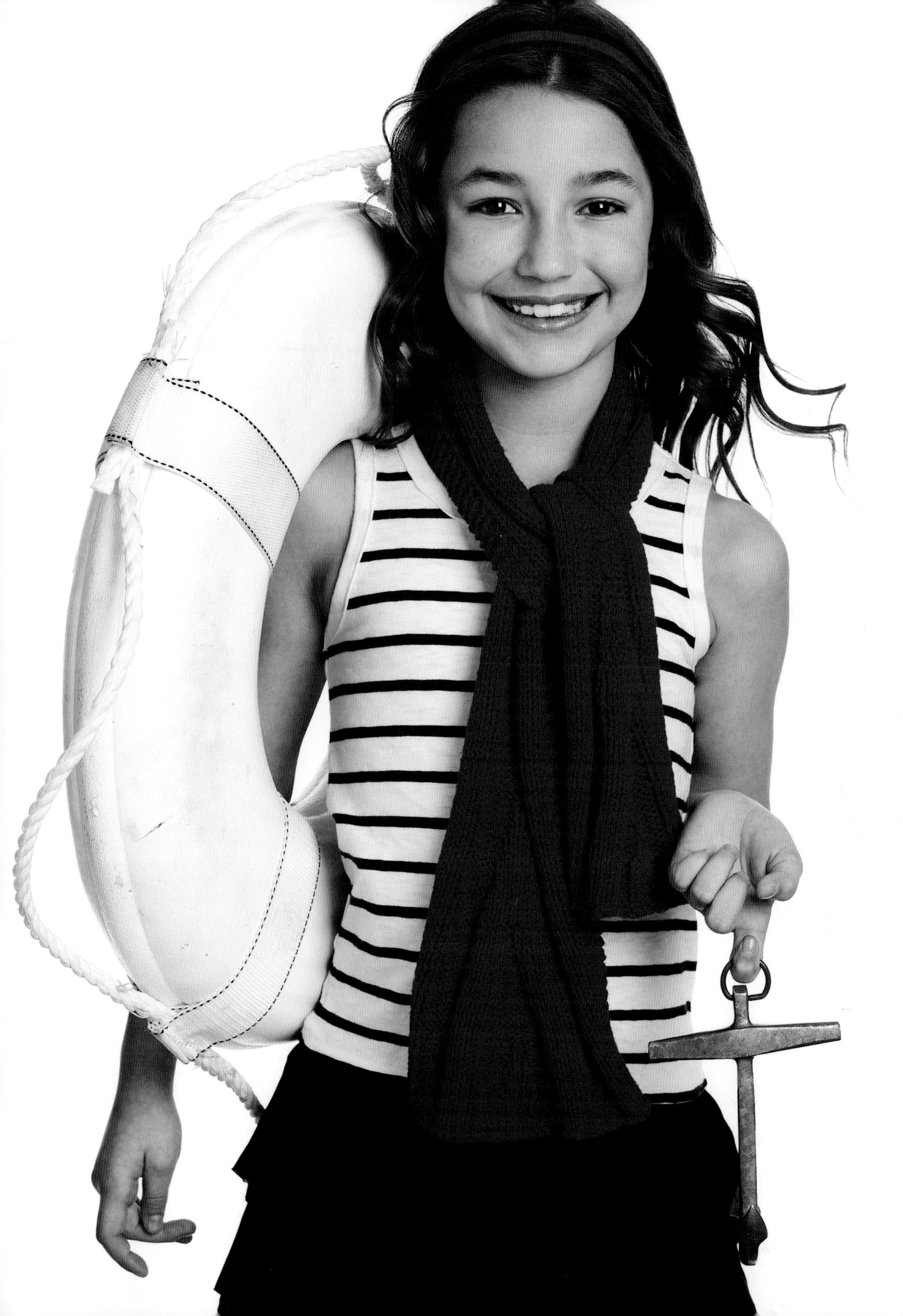

Paul Amato for Lvarepresents.com

CHEVRON
scarf

CHART 2
end with 55 sts

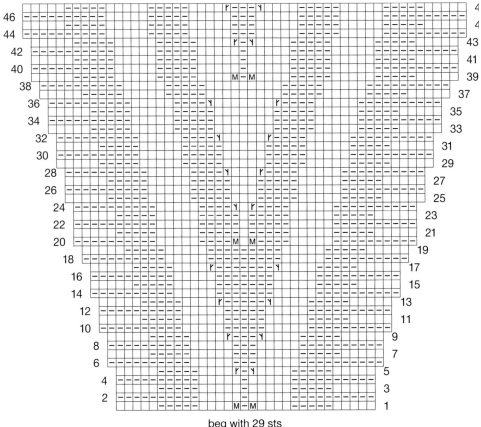

beg with 29 sts

STITCH KEY

□ k on RS, p on WS	⊠ k2tog	⅄ SK2P	Ⴤ pbkf	
⊟ p on RS, k on WS	⊠ SKP	Ⓜ M1	Ⴤ kfb	

EMBROIDERED
pullover

MATERIALS
Yarn
- 8¾oz/250g, 630yd/580m
  (8¾oz/250g, 630yd/580m;
  10½oz/300g, 750yd/690m;
  12¼oz/350g, 880yd/810m) of any
  DK weight
  cotton yarn in white (MC)
- 1¾oz/50g, 130yd/120m in red (CC)

Needles
- One pair size 4 (3.5mm) needles
  or size to obtain gauge

Notions
- Size E/4 (3.5mm) crochet hook
- Stitch holder
- Yarn needle

SIZES
Sized for girl's 8 (10, 12, 14). Shown in
size 8.

MEASUREMENTS
Chest 31 (33, 35, 36½)"/78.5 (84, 89,
92.5)cm
Length 14 (15, 17, 18½)"/36 (38, 43, 47)
cm
Upper arm 11½ (12¼, 13, 13¾)"/29
(31, 33, 35)cm

GAUGE
22 sts and 42 rows to 4"/10cm over
garter st using size 4 (3.5mm) needles
Take time to check your gauge.

BACK
With MC, cast on 86 (90, 96, 100) sts.
Work even in garter st (k every row)
until piece measures 8¼ (8½, 10¼,
11½)"/21 (22, 26, 29)cm.

Shape armholes
Bind off 3 (4, 5, 6) sts at beg of next 2

Seppo Saarentola/Moda

rows, 2 sts at beg of next 2 rows, then
dec 1 st each side on every other row
4 times—68 (70, 74, 76) sts. Work
even until armhole measures 5 (5½, 6,
6¼)"/13 (14, 15, 16)cm.

Shape neck
Next row (RS) Work first 23 (23, 25, 25)
sts, join a 2nd ball of yarn and bind off
22 (24, 24, 26) sts, work to end. Working
both sides at once, bind off 4 sts at each
neck edge once, then 2 sts at each neck
edge once—17 (17, 19, 19) sts. Work

even until armhole measures 6 (6¼, 6½,
7)"/15 (16, 17, 18)cm. Bind off.

FRONT
Work as for back until armhole measures 2¾ (3¼, 3½, 4)"/7 (8, 9, 10)cm.

Shape center opening
and neck
Next row (RS) Work first 34 (35, 37, 38)
sts, join a 2nd ball of yarn and work to
end. Working both sides at once, work
even until center opening measures

EMBROIDERED
pullover

1½"/4cm. Bind off 9 (10, 10, 11) sts at each neck edge once, then 2 sts at each neck edge 4 times—17 (17, 19, 19) sts. Work even until armhole measures same as back to shoulders. Bind off.

SLEEVES
Shape vent
With MC, cast on 22 (23, 24, 25) sts. Work even in garter st until piece measures 1¼"/3cm from beg. Place sts on stitch holder. Make another piece in same way.

Next row Work across, pick up sts from holder and k—44 (46, 48, 50) sts. Work even in garter st until sleeve measures 1½ (2, 2, 2½)"/4 (5, 5, 6)cm, inc 1 st each side on next row and then every 10th row 9 (10, 11, 12) times more—64 (68, 72, 76) sts. Work even until sleeve measures 11¾ (12½, 13½, 15)"/30 (32, 34, 38)cm from beg.

Shape cap
Bind off 3 (4, 5, 6) sts at beg of next 2 rows, 2 sts at beg of next 6 rows, 1 st at each side on every other row 14 (15, 16, 17) times, then bind off 2 sts at beg of next 2 rows—14 sts. If necessary, work even until cap measures measures 3½ (3¾, 4, 4¼)"/9 (9.5, 10, 10.5)cm. Bind off.

FINISHING
Sew shoulder seams. With MC, work 1 rnd sc around neckline, followed by 1 rnd sl st. Sew side and sleeve seams, leaving 1½"/3cm at lower edge of each side seam open. With yarn needle and CC, embroider a line of running stitches, weaving under and over 1 st, around neckline, lower edge and sleeve edges. With CC, embroider a flower at each side of neck, each side of sleeve vent and each sleeve vents at lower edge of sleeve. For each flower, work four

¾"/2cm straight stitches that cross each other, then make a small cross stitch over the intersection of the first 4 stitches. See how-to below. ■

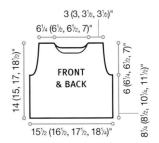

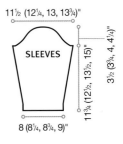

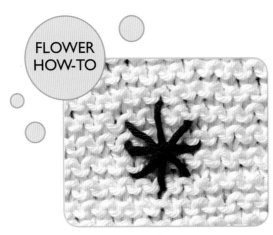

To embroider flowers, make ¾"/2cm straight stitches, crossing them as shown.

Embroider a cross-stitch over the intersection of the first 4 stitches to secure the center of the flower.

PUFFY dress

SIZES
Sized for Girl's 4, 6, 8. Shown in size 4.

MEASUREMENTS
Chest 24 (27, 30)"/61(68.5, 76)cm
Length 25½ (26½, 27½)"/64.5 (67.5, 70)cm
Upper arm 10 (11, 12)"/25.5 (28, 30.5)cm

GAUGE
17 sts and 25 rows to 4"/10cm over St st using larger needles.
Take time to check your gauge.

SEED STITCH
Row 1 (RS) *K1, p1; rep from * to end,
Row 2 Knit the p sts and purl the k sts.
Rep row 2 for seed st.

BACK
With smaller needles, cast on 116 (128, 140) sts. Work in seed st for 1"/2.5cm, end with a WS row. Change to larger needles and cont in St st until piece measures 12 (12½, 13)"/30.5 (31.5, 33)cm from beg, end with a WS row.
Dec row (RS) K2, ssk, k to last 4 sts, k2tog, k2. Rep dec row every 6th row 5 times more, end with a WS row—104 (116, 128) sts.
Next (dec) row (RS) *K2tog; rep from * to end—52 (58, 64) sts. Work even until piece measures 20½ (21, 21½)"/52 (53.5, 54.5)cm from beg, end with a WS row.

Shape armholes
Bind off 3 (3, 4) sts at beg of next 2 rows.
Next (dec) row (RS) K2, ssk, k to last 4 sts, k2tog, k2. Purl next row. Rep last 2 rows 2 (3, 3) times more—40 (44, 48) sts. Work even until armhole measures 5 (5½, 6)"/12.5 (14, 15)cm, end with a WS row. Bind off.

FRONT
Work as for back until armhole measures 3 (3½, 4)"/7.5 (9, 10)cm, end with a WS row—40 (44, 48) sts.

Shape neck
Next row (RS) Work across first 13 (14, 16) sts, join a 2nd ball of yarn and bind off center 14 (16, 16) sts, work to end. Working both sides at once, work next row even.
Next (dec) row (RS) With first ball of yarn, k to last 3 sts, k2tog, k1; with 2nd ball of yarn, k1, ssk, k to end. Purl next row. Rep last 2 rows 3 times more. Work even on 9 (10, 12) sts each side until piece measures same length as back to shoulder, end with a WS row. Bind off rem sts each side for shoulders.

SLEEVES
With smaller needles, cast on 32 (36, 40) sts. Work in seed st for ¾"/2cm, end with a WS row. Change to larger needles.

Next (inc) row (RS) K2 (3, 5), *M1, k3; rep from * 9 (10, 10) times more, end k0 (0, 2)—42 (47, 51) sts. Beg with a purl row, cont in St st until piece measures 3"/7.5cm from beg, end with a WS row.

Shape cap
Bind off 3 (3, 4) sts at beg of next 2 rows.
Next (dec) row (RS) K2, ssk, k to last 4 sts, k2tog, k2. Purl next row. Rep last 2 rows 2 (3, 3) times more—30 (33, 35) sts. Work even until cap measures 3 (3½, 4)"/7.5 (9, 10)cm, end with a WS row.
Next (dec) row (RS) K0 (1, 1), *k2tog; rep from * to end. Bind off rem 15 (17, 18) sts purlwise.

FINISHING
Block pieces to measurements. Sew shoulder seams. Set in sleeves. Sew side and sleeve seams.

Neck edging
With RS facing and crochet hook, join yarn with a sl st in left shoulder seam.
Rnd 1 (RS) Ch 1, making sure that work lies flat, sc evenly around entire neck edge, join rnd with a sl st in first st.
Rnd 2 *Sl st in next 2 sts, ch 3; rep from * around, join rnd with a sl st in first st. Fasten off.

Belt loops (make 2)
With crochet hook, make a chain 1¾"/4.5cm long. Fasten off. Sew each belt loop to side seams, just above top of skirt.

Ribbon embellishment
Cut a 60 (64, 67)"/152.5 (162.5, 170)cm length of ribbon; set aside for sash belt. Thread one end of rem ribbon into a large-eye yarn needle. With RS of back of dress facing, beg approx 3"/7.5cm from left side seam and 2½"/6.5cm from lower edge. Weave needle under and through

MATERIALS
Yarn (4)
• 14oz/400g, 800yd/740m (17½oz/500g, 1000yd/920m; 19¼oz/550g, 1100yd/1010m) of any worsted weight wool yarn in light pink

Needles
• One pair each sizes 7 and 8 (4.5 and 5mm) needles *or size to obtain gauge*

Notions
• Size G/6 (4mm) crochet hook
• 4¼ (4½, 4¾)yd/4 (4.25, 4.5)m of 2½"/63mm wide ribbon silk ribbon
• Matching sewing thread
• Sewing needle
• Large-eye yarn needle

2 sts. Draw ribbon through leaving a 4"/10cm end. Use both ribbon ends to tie a loose knot. For next knot, weave needle under and through 2 sts at left side seam, 3"/7.5cm from bottom edge. Draw ribbon through leaving a 3"/7.5cm long loop. Use needle end of ribbon, tie a loose knot. Referring to photo, cont to work in this manner, changing height and spacing of knots and length of loops to within 2½"/6.5cm of right side seam and 6½"/165cm from bottom edge. Trim ribbon ends at an angle. On WS, tack knots to secure using sewing needle and thread. ■

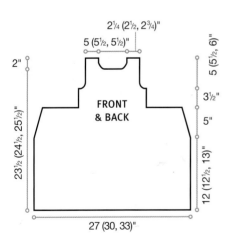

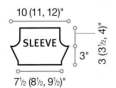

GIRL'S dress

SIZES
Sized for girl's 8 (10, 12, 14). Shown in size 8.

MEASUREMENTS
Chest 28½ (30, 32, 33)"/72 (76, 82, 84)cm
Length 25½ (28, 29½, 30½)"/65 (71, 75, 80)cm
Upper arm 9½ (9¾, 11, 11½)"/24 (25, 28, 29)cm

GAUGE
22 sts and 28 rows to 4"/10cm over St st using size 4 (3.5mm) needles
Take time to check your gauge.

NOTES
1 Dress is knit in one piece in rnds from skirt to armholes. Work is then divided for front and back with each piece being worked separately from that point on.
2 When working drop stitch pattern, be sure that strands from unraveled sts are on WS of work.
3 Be careful that picked-up CC sts do not become twisted.
4 See inset on next page for stitch details.

STITCH GLOSSARY
St st in rnds K every rnd.

DROP STITCH PATTERN IN RNDS
(multiple of 3 sts)
Rnd 1 With CC, purl.
Rnds 2 and 3 With MC, knit.
Rnd 4 *With MC, *k2, with RH needle and from back to front, pick up right edge of next CC st 2 rows below, drop next MC st off LH needle and unravel 2 MC rows, place CC st on LH needle and knit; rep from * to end.

MATERIALS
Yarn ③
• 15¾oz/450g, 1130yd/1040m (17½oz/500g, 1250yd/1150m; 17½oz/500g, 1250yd/1150m; 19¼oz/550g, 1380yd/1270m) of any DK weight cotton yarn in red (MC)
• 1¾oz/50g, 130yd/120m in white (CC)

Needles
• Size 4 (3.5mm) circular knitting needles, 20"/50cm long *or size to obtain gauge*

Notions
• Large stitch holder

Rnds 5 and 6 With MC, knit. Rep rows 1–6 for pat st.

DROP STITCH PATTERN IN ROWS
(multiple of 3 sts plus 2)
Row 1 (WS) With CC, knit. Move sts to opposite end of needle and pick up MC.
Row 2 (WS) With MC, purl. Turn.
Row 3 (RS) With MC, knit. Turn.
Row 4 (WS) With MC, *p2, with RH needle and from back to front, pick up right edge of next CC st 2 rows below, drop next MC st off LH needle and unravel 2 MC rows, place CC st on LH, with MC, purl the CC st; rep from * to end. Turn.
Row 5 (RS) With MC, knit. Turn.
Row 6 (WS) With MC, purl. Turn.
Row 7 (RS) With CC, purl. Move sts to opposite end of needle and pick up MC.
Row 8 (RS) With MC, knit. Turn.
Row 9 (WS) With MC, purl.
Row 10 (RS) With MC, *k2, with RH needle and from back to front, pick up right edge of next CC st 2 rows below, drop next MC st off LH needle and unravel 2 MC rows, place CC st on LH needle and knit; rep from * to last 2 sts, k2. Turn.

Row 11 (WS) With MC, purl.
Row 12 (RS) With MC, knit. Rep rows 1–12 for pat st.

SKIRT/BODICE
Hem With MC and circular needle, cast on 216 (228, 240, 252) sts. Join ends being careful not to twist sts. Work even for 5 rnds in St st.
Turning rnd Purl. Work even in St st until piece measures 6½ (6½, 6, 5½)"/17 (17, 15, 14)cm from turning rnd.
Dec rnd *K16 (17, 18, 19), k2tog; rep from * around—204 (216, 228, 240) sts. Work even until piece measures 8½ (9, 8¾, 8¾)"/21.5 (23, 22, 22)cm from turning rnd.
Next dec rnd *K15 (16, 17, 18), k2tog; rep from * around—192 (204, 216, 228) sts. Work even until piece measures 10½ (11½, 11½, 12)"/26.5 (29, 29, 30.5)cm from turning rnd.
Next dec rnd Dec 12 sts as before, having one less st between decs on every dec rnd. Rep dec rnd twice more having 2 (2¼, 2¾, 3¼)"/5 (6, 7, 8)cm between each dec rnd—156 (168, 180, 192) sts. Work even until piece measures 15¼ (17, 17¾, 19)"/39 (43, 45, 48)cm from turning rnd. Change to drop st pat and work even in rnds until piece measures 19¾ (21½, 22¾, 24½)"/50 (55, 58, 62)cm from turning rnd.

Divide for front and back
Bind off 4 sts, work in pat for 72 (78, 84, 90) sts for front, bind off 6 sts for armhole, work in pat for 72 (78, 84, 90) sts for back, bind off 2 sts. Place front sts on a stitch holder.

Shape armholes and back neck
Note As you shape armholes, be sure to keep CC drop stitch sts lined up as established.

20

Seppo Saarentola/Moda

GIRL'S dress

Cont in drop st pat, working back and forth in rows, bind off 2 sts at beg of next 2 rows, then dec 1 st each side every other row 2 (3, 4, 5) times—64 (68, 72, 76) sts. Work even until armhole measures 5 (5½, 6, 6¼)"/13 (14, 15, 16) cm, end with a WS row.
Work in pat over first 18 (20, 21, 23) sts, join a 2nd ball of yarn, bind off 28 (28, 30, 30) sts for back neck, work in pat to end. Working both sides at once, work 2 rows even, then bind off 4 sts at each neck edge. Bind off rem 14 (16, 17, 19) sts for each shoulder.

FRONT
Pick up front stitches from holder. Work as for back until armhole measures 3¼ (3½, 3½, 4)"/8 (9, 9, 10)cm, end with a WS row. Work in pat over first 26 (28, 29, 31) sts, join a 2nd ball of yarn and bind off 12 (12, 14, 14) sts for back neck, work to end. Bind off 3 sts at each neck edge twice, then 2 sts at each neck, then dec 1 st every other row 4 times—14 (16, 17, 19) sts. Work even until armhole measures same as back. Bind off.

SLEEVES
With MC, cast on 50 (52, 54, 56) sts.
Hem Work even in St st for 5 rows.
Turning row (WS) Knit. Work even in St st, inc 1 st each side every 8th (8th, 4th, 3rd) row 1 (1, 3, 4) times—52 (54, 60, 64) sts. Work even until sleeve measures 2"/5cm from turning row, end with a WS row.

Shape cap
Bind off 5 sts at beg of next 2 rows, 2 sts at beg of next 6 rows, dec 1 st each side every other row 8 (8, 9, 10) times, bind off 2 sts at beg of next 2 rows—10 (12, 16, 18) sts. Work even until cap measures 3½ (3½, 4, 4¼)"/9 (9, 10, 11) cm. Bind off.

FINISHING
Sew one shoulder seam.

Neckband
With MC and RS facing, pick up and k 102 (104, 108, 108) sts around neckline; work in St st for 4 rows; k 1 row on WS for turning row; k 5 rows in St st. Bind off. Sew rem shoulder and neck edge seam. Fold neckband in half to WS and sew in place. Set in sleeves and sew sleeve seams. Fold sleeve and lower edge hems to WS and sew in place. ■

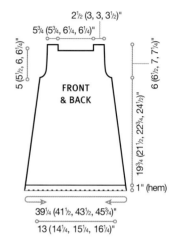

2½ (3, 3, 3½)"
5¾ (5¾, 6¼, 6¼)"
5 (5½, 6, 6¼)"
FRONT & BACK
6 (6½, 7, 7¼)"
19¾ (21½, 22¾, 24½)"
1" (hem)
39¼ (41½, 43½, 45¾)"
13 (14¼, 15¼, 16¼)"

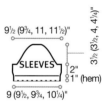

9½ (9¾, 11, 11½)"
3½ (3½, 4, 4¼)"
SLEEVES
2"
1" (hem)
9 (9½, 9¾, 10¼)"

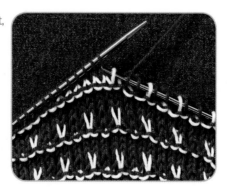

Pick up the right side of the next white stitch 2 rows below, inserting the needle from back to front.

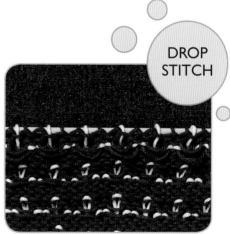

The 2 rows of red stitches above the white stitch are unraveled, as shown here on the WS of the work.

DROP STITCH

KERCHIEF

MATERIALS

Yarn
- 3½oz/100g, 210yd/200m of any worsted weight acrylic and cotton blend yarn each in red (A) and white (B)

Needles
- One pair size 7 (4.5mm) needles *or size to obtain gauge*
- Two size 7 (4.5mm) double-pointed needles (dpns)

MEASUREMENTS
13 x 8"/33 x 20.5cm

GAUGE
18 sts and 38 rows to 4"/10cm over garter st using size 7 (4.5mm) needles. *Take time to check your gauge.*

STRIPE PATTERN
*2 rows A, 2 rows B; rep from * (4 rows) for stripe pat.

KERCHIEF
With A, cast on 59 sts. Work in garter st (k every row) and stripe pat as foll:
Work 2 rows even.
Dec 1 st each side on next row and rep dec every alternate 4th and 2nd row until 3 sts rem. K3tog. Fasten off last st.

I-cord ties (make 2)
With dpns and A, cast on 3 sts.
Next row (RS) K3. Do not turn. Slide to beg of needle to work next row from RS.
Rep from * for approx 17"/43cm, or desired length. K3tog and fasten off last st. Attach tie to each end of kerchief. ▪

Paul Amato for Lvarepresents.com

CABLED jumper

SIZES
Sized for Girl's 2, 4, 6, 8 years. Shown in size 4.

MEASUREMENTS
Chest 23 (24, 25, 26)"/58.5 (61, 63.5, 66)cm
Length 22¼ (24, 26¼, 30)"/56.5 (61, 66.5, 76)cm

GAUGE
23 sts and 32 rows/rnds to 4"/10cm over St st (stretched slightly) using size 7 (4.5mm) needles.
Take time to check your gauge.

STITCH GLOSSARY
4-st LC Sl 2 sts to cn and hold to *front*, k2, k2 from cn.
4-st RC Sl 2 sts to cn and hold to *back*, k2, k2 from cn.
3-st LPC Sl 2 sts to cn and hold to *front*, p1, k2 from cn.
3-st RPC Sl 1 st to cn and hold to *back*, k2, p1 from cn.
5-st RPC Sl 3 sts to cn and hold to *back*, k2, slip the purl st back to LH needle and p1, k2 from cn.
5-st LPC Sl 3 sts to cn and hold to *front*, k2, slip the purl st back to LH needle and p1, k2 from cn.

MATERIALS

Yarn (3)
- 8¾oz/250g, 500yd/460m (8¾oz/250g, 500yd/460m; 10½oz/300g, 600yd/550m; 12¼oz/350g, 700yd/640m) in any DK weight cotton yarn in turquoise

Needles
- One size 7 (4.5mm) circular needle, 24"/60cm long *or size to obtain gauge*
- One set (5) size 7 (4.5mm) double-pointed needles (dpns)

Notions
- Cable needles (cn)
- Stitch holders

CABLE BAND
Cast on 23 sts.
Row 1 (WS) K5, p2, k2, p5, k2, p2, k5.

Beg chart
Beg with row 2 (RS), cont to foll chart for cable band until band measures approx 22 (23, 24, 25)"/56 (58.5, 61, 63.5)cm. Bind off. Sew the ends tog to form the waistband.

BODICE
With RS facing, pick up and k 120 (126, 132, 138) sts around the top edge of the waistband. Join and cont to work in rnds as foll:

Rnd 1 K60 (63, 66, 69), place marker (pm), k to end of rnd, pm to mark beg of rnd. Cont in St st (k every rnd) for 4 rnds more.
Inc rnd Inc 1 st in first st, k to 1 st before marker, inc 1 st in next st, sl marker, inc 1 st in next st, k to last st, inc 1 st in last st—4 sts inc'd. Rep inc rnd every 6th rnd twice more—132 (138, 144, 150) sts. Work even until bodice measures 2½ (3, 4, 6)"/6.5 (7.5, 10, 15)cm from the pick up line, end at 6 sts before the end of the last rnd.

Shape armhole
Bind off 12 sts, removing marker, k to 6 sts before next marker, bind off 12 sts, removing marker, k to end.

FRONT
Working back and forth in rows, on the 54 (57, 60, 63) sts for front only, purl 1 row.
Dec row (RS) K1, SKP, k to last 3 sts, k2tog, k1. Rep dec row every other row 5 times more—42 (45, 48, 51) sts. Work even until armhole measures 1¾ (2, 2¼, 2½)"/4.5 (5, 6, 6.5)cm.

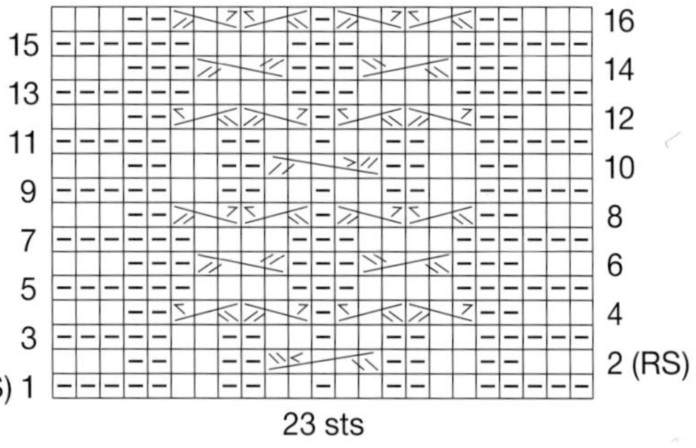

16
15
14
13
12
11
10
9
8
7
6
5
4
3
2 (RS)
(WS) 1
23 sts

STITCH KEY
- □ k on RS, p on WS
- ⊟ p on RS, k on WS
- 4-st RC
- 4-st LC
- 3-st LPC
- 3-st RPC
- 5-st RPC
- 5-st LPC

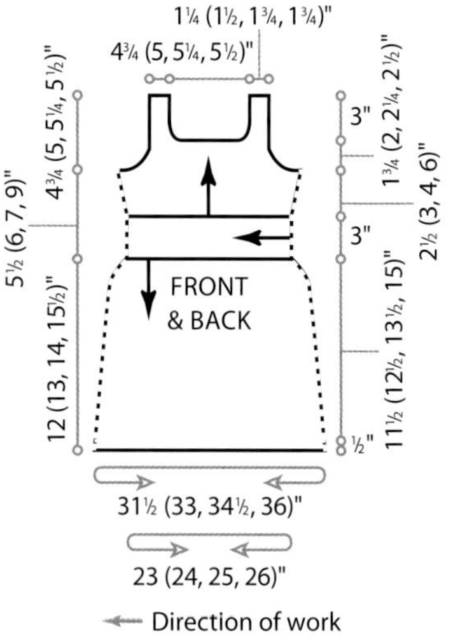

1¼ (1½, 1¾, 1¾)"
4¾ (5, 5¼, 5½)"
4¾ (5, 5¼, 5½)"
5½ (6, 7, 9)"
3"
1¾ (2, 2¼, 2½)"
2½ (3, 4, 6)"
3"
FRONT & BACK
12 (13, 14, 15½)"
11½ (12½, 13½, 15)"
½"
31½ (33, 34½, 36)"
23 (24, 25, 26)"
Direction of work

Shape neck

Next row (RS) K11 (12, 13, 14), join a 2nd ball of yarn and bind off center 20 (21, 22, 23) sts, k to end. Working both sides at once, dec 1 st at each neck edge every other row 4 times—7 (8, 9, 10) sts each side. Work even until armhole measures 4¾ (5, 5¼, 5½)"/12 (12.5, 13.5, 14) cm. Place sts each side on holders.

BACK

Rejoin yarn to work the back sts, and work same as for front.

SKIRT

Pick up and k 120 (126, 132, 138) sts around the lower edge of the waistband.
Rnd 1 Knit, pm for beg of rnd.
Inc rnd *K1, inc 1 st in next st; rep from * around—180 (189, 198, 207) sts. Cont in St st (k every rnd) until skirt measures 11½ (12½, 13½, 15)"/29 (32, 34, 38)cm. [P 1 rnd, k 1 rnd] 3 times. Bind off.

FINISHING

Join the shoulders tog using 3-needle bind-off method. (See page 28.)

Armhole trims

With RS facing and dpn, pick up and k 58 (62, 65, 68) sts evenly around armhole edge. Join and p 1 rnd. Bind off knitwise.

Neck trim

With RS facing and dpn, pick up and k 112 (114, 116, 118) sts evenly around neck edge. Join and p 1 rnd. Bind off knitwise. ■

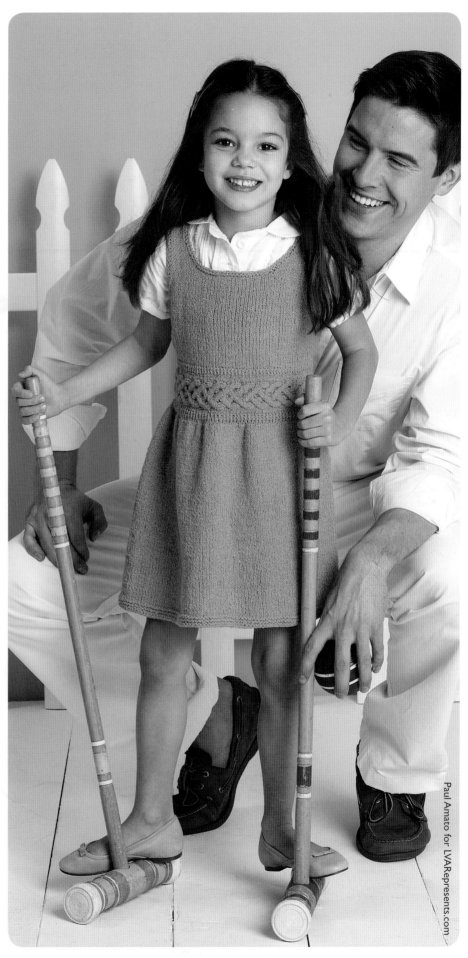

FLYAWAY
cardi

SIZES
Sized for 9 months, 1, 2, 3 years. Shown in size 2 years.

MEASUREMENTS
Chest (closed) 23 (25, 27, 29)"/58.5 (63.5, 68.5, 73.5)cm
Length 11½ (12½, 13, 14)"/28 (30.5, 33, 35.5)cm
Upper arm 10 (11, 12, 13)"/25.5 (28, 30.5, 33)cm

GAUGE
18 sts and 24 rows to 4"/10cm over St st using larger needles.
Take time to check your gauge.

BACK
With smaller needles, cast on 62 (66, 74, 80) sts. K next 3 (3, 5, 5) rows, end with a WS row. Change to larger needles and St st and work for 6 (8, 8, 10) rows.

Shape sides
Dec row (RS) K4, ssk, k to last 6 sts, k2tog, k2. Rep dec row every 6th row 4 (4, 5, 6) times more—52 (56, 62, 66) sts. Work even until piece measures 6½ (7½, 9, 10½)"/16.5 (19, 23, 26.5)cm from beg, end with a WS row.

Shape raglan armholes
Bind off 4 (4, 5, 5) sts at beg of next 2 rows. Place rem 44 (48, 52, 56) sts on holder.

LEFT FRONT
With smaller needles, cast on 34 (36, 40, 43) sts. K next 3 (3, 5, 5) rows, end with a WS row. Change to larger needles.
Next row (RS) K30 (32, 36, 39), pm, k4.
Next row K4, p to end. Keeping 4 sts at front edge in garter st, cont to work even for 4 (6, 6, 8) rows.

MATERIALS
Yarn ④
• 7oz/200g, 400yd/370m (8¾oz/250g, 500yd/460m; 10½oz/300g, 600yd550m; 12¼oz/350g, 700yd/640m) of any worsted weight wool blend yarn in light pink

Needles
• One pair each sizes 7 and 8 (4.5 and 5mm) needles
or size to obtain gauge
• Size 8 (8mm) circular needle, 24"/60cm long

Notions
• Stitch holders
• Stitch markers
• Two ⁹⁄₁₆"/14mm buttons

Shape side
Dec row (RS) K4, ssk, k to end. Rep dec row every 6th row 4 (4, 5, 6) times more—29 (31, 34, 36) sts. Work even until piece measures same length as back to underarm, end with a WS row.

Shape raglan armhole
Bind off 4 (4, 5, 5) sts, work to end. Work next row even. Place rem 25 (27, 29, 31) sts on holder.

RIGHT FRONT
With smaller needles, cast on 34 (36, 40, 43) sts. K next 3 (3, 5, 5) rows, end with a WS row. Change to larger needles.
Next row (RS) K4, pm, k to end.
Next row P to marker, k4. Keeping 4 sts at front edge in garter st, cont to work even for 4 (6, 6, 8) rows.

Shape side
Dec row (RS) K to last 6 sts, k2tog, k4. Rep dec row every 6th row 4 (4, 5, 6) times more—29 (31, 34, 36) sts.

Work even until piece measures same length as back to underarm, end with a RS row.

Shape raglan armhole
Bind off 4 (4, 5, 5) sts, work to end. Place rem 25 (27, 29, 31) sts on holder.

SLEEVES
With smaller needles, cast on 32 (32, 34, 34) sts. K next 3 (3, 5, 5) rows, end with a WS row. Change to larger needles. Cont in St st until piece measures 1 (1, 1½, 1½)"/2.5 (2.5, 4, 4)cm from beg, end with a WS row.
Inc row (RS) K3, M1, k to last 3 sts, M1, k3. Rep inc row every 4th row 6 (8, 9, 11) times more—46 (50, 54, 58) sts. Work even until piece measures 6 (7, 8½ 10)"/15 (17.5, 21.5, 25.5)cm from beg, end with a WS row.

Shape raglan cap
Bind off 4 (4, 5, 5) sts at beg of next 2 rows. Place rem 38 (42, 44, 48) sts on holder.

YOKE
With RS facing and circular needle, k25 (27, 29, 31) sts from right front holder, pm, 38 (42, 44, 48) sts from sleeve holder, pm, 44 (48, 52, 56) sts from back holder, pm, 38 (42, 44, 48) sts from sleeve holder, pm, 25 (27, 29, 31) sts from left front holder—170 (186, 198, 214) sts.
Do not join.
Keeping 4 sts each front edge in garter st, work back and forth for 3 (3, 1, 1) rows, end with a WS row.

Shape raglan armholes
Dec row (RS) K4, sl marker, [k to 3 sts before next marker, k2tog, k1, sl marker, k2, ssk] twice, [k to 4 sts before next marker, k2tog, k2, sl marker, k1, ssk] twice,

k to end. Rep dec row every other row 1 (3, 4, 6) times more, end with a WS row.

Buttonhole (dec) row (RS) K1, k2tog, yo, k1, [k to 3 sts before next marker, k2tog, k1, sl marker, k2, ssk] twice, [k to 4 sts before next marker, k2tog, k2, sl marker, k1, ssk] twice, k to end.

Work next row even. Rep dec row on next row, then every other row 6 times more, end with a WS row. Rep buttonhole row. Work next row even. Rep dec row on next row, then every other row once more, end with a WS row—66 (66, 70, 70) sts.

Neckband

K next 3 (3, 5, 5) rows. Bind off all sts knitwise.

FINISHING

Block piece to measurements. Sew bound-off sts of raglan caps to bound-off sts of raglan armholes. Sew side and sleeve seams. Sew on buttons. ◼

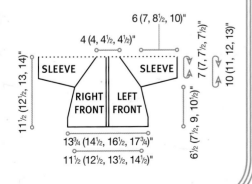

Rose Callahan

CROPPED top

SIZES
Sized for Child 2 (4, 6, 8, 10, 12). Shown in size 6.

MEASUREMENTS
Chest 22 (23½, 25½, 27½, 29½, 31)"/56 (58, 65, 70, 75, 78.5)cm
Length 11 (12, 13, 15, 16½, 17½)"/28 (30.5, 33, 38, 42, 44.5)cm

GAUGE
17 sts and 19 rows to 4"/10cm over k1, p1 rib using size 10 (6mm) needles.
Take time to check your gauge.

3-NEEDLE BIND-OFF
1 Hold right sides of pieces together on two needles. Insert third needle knitwise into first st of each needle, and wrap yarn knitwise.
2 Knit these two sts together, and slip them off the needles. *Knit the next two sts together in the same manner.
3 Slip first st on 3rd needle over 2nd st and off needle. Rep from * in step 2 across row until all sts are bound off.

BACK
With size 10 (6mm) needles, cast on 67 (73, 79, 85, 91, 97) sts. Work in seed st as foll:
Row 1 (RS) K1, *p1, k1; rep from * to end.
Row 2 K the purl sts and p the knit sts.
Rep row 2 for seed st until piece measures 2½"/6.5cm from beg, end with a WS row.
Next (dec) row (RS) K1, *k2tog, k1; rep from * to end—45 (49, 53, 57, 61, 65) sts.
Row 1 (WS) K1, [k1, p1] 9 (10, 11, 12, 13, 14) times, k7, [p1, k1] 9 (10, 11, 12, 13, 14) times, k1.

MATERIALS
Yarn (5)
• 7oz/200g, 220yd/210m (7oz/200g, 220yd/210m; 7oz/200g, 220yd/210m; 10½oz/300g, 330yd/310m; 10½oz/300g, 330yd/310m; 10½oz/300g, 330yd/310m) of any bulky weight cotton yarn in light blue
Needles
• One pair size 10 (6mm) needles *or size to obtain gauge*
Notion
• Stitch holders

Row 2 K1, [p1, k1] 9 (10, 11, 12, 13, 14) times, k7, [k1, p1] 9 (10, 11, 12, 13, 14) times, k1.
Rep the last 2 rows until piece measures 6 (6½, 7, 9, 10, 10½)"/15 (16.5, 18, 23, 25.5, 26.5)cm from beg, end with a WS row.

Armhole shaping
Bind off 2 (2, 2, 3, 3, 3) sts at beg of next 2 rows.
Next row (RS) K1, k2tog, work to last 3 sts, SKP, k1.
Next row K1, work to last st, k1.
Rep the last 2 rows 2 (2, 2, 2, 3, 3) times more—35 (39, 43, 45, 47, 51) sts.
Work even until armhole measures 3¼ (3¾ 4¼, 4¼, 4¾, 5)"/8 (9.5, 11, 11.5, 12, 12.5)cm, end with a RS row.

Neck shaping
Next row (WS) Work 12 (13, 14, 15, 15, 17) sts, join a 2nd ball of yarn and bind off center 11 (13, 15, 15, 17, 17) sts, work to end.
Working both sides at once, dec 1 st at each neck edge every row 5 times—7 (8, 9, 10, 10, 12) sts.
Work even until armhole measures 5 (5½, 6, 6, 6½, 7)"/13 (14, 15, 15, 16.5,

18)cm, end with a WS row. Leave rem sts each side for shoulder on holder.

FRONT
Work same as for back until armhole measures 1¼ (1¾, 2, 2, 2¼, 3)"/3 (4.5, 5, 5.5, 6.5, 7.5)cm, end with a RS row.

Neck shaping
Next row (WS) Work 13 (15, 16, 17, 17, 19) sts, join a 2nd ball of yarn and bind off center 9 (9, 11, 11, 13, 13) sts, work to end.
Working both sides at once, dec 1 st at each neck edge every row 4 times, then every other row 2 (3, 3, 3, 3, 3) times—7 (8, 9, 10, 10, 12) sts.
Work even until armhole measures same as back. Leave rem sts each side for shoulder on holder.

FINISHING
Join shoulder seams with 3-needle bind-off. Sew side seams. ■

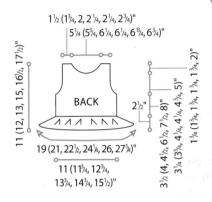

1 1/2 (1 3/4, 2, 2 1/4, 2 1/4, 2 3/4)"

5 1/4 (5 3/4, 6 1/4, 6 1/4, 6 3/4, 6 3/4)"

11 (12, 13, 15, 16 1/2, 17 1/2)"

BACK

2 1/2"

3 1/4 (3 3/4, 4 1/4, 4 3/4, 5)"

1 3/4 (1 3/4, 1 3/4, 1 3/4, 2)"

19 (21, 22 1/2, 24 1/4, 26, 27 3/4)"

11 (11 3/4, 12 3/4, 13 3/4, 14 3/4, 15 1/2)"

3 1/2 (4, 4 1/2, 6 1/2, 7 1/2, 8)"

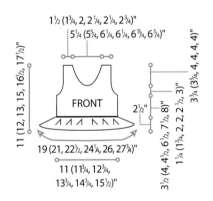

1 1/2 (1 3/4, 2, 2 1/4, 2 1/4, 2 3/4)"

5 1/4 (5 3/4, 6 1/4, 6 1/4, 6 3/4, 6 3/4)"

11 (12, 13, 15, 16 1/2, 17 1/2)"

FRONT

2 1/2"

3 3/4 (3 3/4, 4, 4, 4, 4)"

1 1/4 (1 3/4, 2, 2, 2 1/2, 3)"

19 (21, 22 1/2, 24 1/4, 26, 27 3/4)"

11 (11 3/4, 12 3/4, 13 3/4, 14 3/4, 15 1/2)"

3 1/2 (4, 4 1/2, 6 1/2, 7 1/2, 8)"

STRIPED dress

SIZES
Sized for Child's 2, 4, 6, 8, 10. Shown in size 4.

MEASUREMENTS
Chest 23½ (26, 28, 30, 31½)"/59.5 (66, 71, 76, 80)cm
Length 18½ (20¼, 21¼, 23¼, 24¾)"/47 (51.5, 54, 59, 63)cm

GAUGE
18 sts and 26 rows to 4"/10cm over St st using size 8 (5mm) needles.
Take time to check your gauge.

STRIPE PATTERN A
2 rows A, 4 rows MC, 2 rows A, 6 rows MC, 2 rows A, 2 rows MC, 4 rows A, 2 rows MC, 6 rows A, 2 rows MC.

STRIPE PATTERN B
(over an odd number of sts)
Row 1 (RS) K1 with MC, *k1 with A, k1 with MC; rep from * to end.
Row 2 P1 with MC, *p1 with A, p1 with MC; rep from * to end.
Rep rows 1 and 2 for stripe pattern B.

STRIPE PATTERN B
(over an even number of sts)
Row 1 (RS) *K1 with MC, k1 with A; rep from * to end.
Row 2 *P1 with A, p1 with MC; rep from * to end.
Rep rows 1 and 2 for stripe pattern B.

STRIPE PATTERN C
*2 rows A, 2 rows MC; rep from *.

STRIPED RIB
(multiple of 2 sts plus 1)
Rows 1 and 3 (WS) With A, *p1, k1; rep from * to last st, p1.

Row 2 With A, *k1, p1; rep from * to last st, k1.
Row 4 With MC, *k1, p1; rep from * to last st, k1.
Row 5 With MC, *p1, k1; rep from * to last st, p1.

BACK
Tie MC and A tog. Make a slip knot with A and place on needle. Using long tail cast-on method so that A forms the loops on needle (A on thumb) and MC forms the edge, cast on 115 (127, 135, 145, 155) sts. Work 5 rows in Striped Rib, end with a WS row.
Work in St st following Stripe Pattern A to end of pat.
Next (dec) row (RS) With A, k0 (0, 3, 2, 0), *k2, SKP; rep from * to last 3 (3, 4, 3, 3) sts, k3 (3, 4, 3, 3)—87 (96, 103, 110, 117) sts.
Beg with a WS row, work 3½ (4, 4, 4½, 5)"/9 (10, 10, 11.5, 13)cm following Stripe Pattern B, end with a RS row.
Next row (WS) With MC, purl.
Next (dec) row With MC, k3 (2, 3, 4, 3), *SKP, k3; rep from * to last 4 (4, 5, 6, 4) sts,

SKP, k2 (2, 3, 4, 2)—70 (77, 83, 89, 94) sts. Work 14 (18, 18, 22, 24) rows in St st following Stripe Pattern C, end with a RS row.
Next row With MC, purl.
Next (dec) row With MC, k2 (3, 3, 1, 2), *SKP, k2; rep from * to last 0 (2, 0, 0, 0) sts, k0 (2, 0, 0, 0)—53 (59, 63, 67, 71) sts. Beg with a WS row, work 1 (1, 5, 5, 7) rows in Stripe Pattern B, end with a WS row.

Shape armhole
Cont in Stripe Pattern B, bind off 5 (6, 6, 7, 7) sts at beg of next 2 rows—43 (47, 51, 53, 57) sts. Work even in pat until armhole measures 2¾ (3¼, 3¼, 3¾, 3¾)"/7 (8, 8, 9.5, 9.5)cm, end with a WS row.

Shape neck
Next row (RS) Work 13 (15, 16, 17, 18) sts, join a 2nd ball of yarn and bind off center 17 (17, 19, 19, 21) sts, work to end. Cont in pat, working both sides at once, until armhole measures 5¾ (6¼, 6¼, 6¾, 7¼)"/14.5 (16, 16, 17, 18.5)cm, end with a WS row. Bind off rem 13 (15, 16, 17, 18) sts each side for shoulder.

FRONT
Work as for back until armhole measures 1¾ (2¼, 2¼, 2¾, 2¾)"/4.5 (6, 6, 7, 7)cm, end with a RS row.

Shape neck
Next row (RS) Work 13 (15, 16, 17, 18) sts, join a 2nd ball of yarn and bind off center 17 (17, 19, 19, 21) sts, work to end. Cont in pat, working both sides at once, until armhole measures same as back. Bind off rem 13 (15, 16, 17, 18) sts each side for shoulder.

FINISHING
Block pieces lightly. Sew shoulder and side seams.

Neck edging

With crochet hook and beg at center back, join A with a sl st into st 1 row below bound-off st, work 1 sc into same space, *ch 2, skip 1 bound-off st, 1 sc into next bound-off st 1 row below; rep from * evenly around neck opening. Join with a slip st to first sc. Fasten off.

Armhole edging

Beg at underarm seam, work same as for neck edging. ■

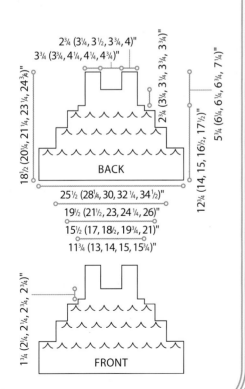

2¾ (3¼, 3½, 3¾, 4)"
3¾ (3¾, 4¼, 4¼, 4¾)"

2¾ (3, 3¼, 3¾, 3¾)"

5¼ (6¼, 6¼, 6¾, 7¼)"

18½ (20¼, 21¼, 23, 24¾)"

12¾ (14, 15, 16½, 17½)"

BACK

25½ (28¼, 30, 32 ¼, 34½)"
19½ (21½, 23, 24 ¼, 26)"
15½ (17, 18½, 19¾, 21)"
11¾ (13, 14, 15, 15¾)"

1¾ (2¼, 2¼, 2¾, 2¾)"

FRONT

SLEEVELESS
dress

SIZES
Sized for Child's 4, 6, 8, 10. Shown in size 6.

MEASUREMENTS
Chest 25 (27, 29, 31)"/63.5 (68.5, 73.5, 78.5)cm
Length 21½ (23, 24½, 26)"/54.5 (58.5, 62, 66)cm

GAUGE
22 sts and 31 rows to 4"/10cm over St st using size 5 (3.75mm) needles.
Take time to check your gauge.

SEED STITCH
(over an odd number of sts)
Row 1 (RS) K1, *p1, k1; rep from * to end.
Row 2 K the purl sts and p the knit sts.
Rep row 2 for seed st.

BACK
With MC, cast on 93 (99, 111, 121) sts.
Work in seed st for 6 (6, 8, 8) rows.
Cont in St st and work even until piece measures 1½"/4cm from beg, end with a WS row.

Shape sides
Dec row (RS) K1, k2tog, knit to last 3 sts, ssk, k1. Rep dec row every 8th row 3 (11, 3, 0) times more, every 6th row 8 (0, 11, 13) times, then every 4th row 0 (0, 0, 4) times—69 (75, 81, 85) sts. Work even until piece measures 12½ (13½, 14½, 15½)"/31.5 (34, 37, 39.5)cm from beg, end with a WS row.

Beg chart pat
Row 1 (RS) Beg with st 4 (1, 4, 2) and work through st 7, work 12-st rep 5 (5, 6, 6) times, then work through st 24 (29, 24, 26). Cont to foll chart in this way through row 16. With MC only, work

MATERIALS
Yarn (4)
• 8¾oz/250g, 690yd/640m (8¾oz/250g, 690yd/640m; 10½oz/300g, 830yd/760m; 12¼oz/300g, 960yd/880m) of any worsted weight wool yarn in pink (MC)
• 1¾oz/50g, 140yd/130m each in cream (A), hot pink (B), and light pink (C)

Needles
• One pair size 5 (3.75mm) needles *or size to obtain guage*

even until piece measures 16 (17, 18, 19)"/40.5 (43, 45.5, 48)cm from beg, end with a WS row.

Shape armholes
Bind off 4 (4, 5, 5) sts at beg of next 2 rows.
Dec row 1 (RS) K1, k2tog, knit to last 3 sts, ssk, k1.
Dec row 2 P1, p2tog tbl, purl to last 3 sts, p2tog, p1. Rep dec row 1 on next row, then every other row 3 times more—49 (55, 59, 63) sts. Work even until armhole measures 4¾ (5¼, 5¾, 6¼)"/12 (13.5, 14.5, 16)cm, end with a WS row.

Shape neck
Next row (RS) K14 (16, 18, 19), join a 2nd ball of MC and bind off center 21 (23, 23, 25) sts, k to end.
Dec row 1 (WS) With first ball of yarn, p to last 3 sts, p2tog tbl, p1; with 2nd ball of yarn, p1, p2tog, p to end.
Dec row 2 (RS) With first ball of yarn, k to last 3 sts, k2tog, k1; with 2nd ball of yarn, k1, ssk, k to end. Rep last 2 rows once more, then dec row 1 once. Work even on 9 (11, 13, 14) sts each side until armhole measures 5½ (6, 6½, 7)"/14 (15, 16.5, 17.5)cm, end with a WS row. Bind off each side for shoulders.

FRONT
Work as for back until armhole measures 2½ (3, 3½, 4)"/6.5 (7.5, 9, 10)cm, end with a WS row.

Shape neck
Next row (RS) K18 (20, 22, 23), join a 2nd ball of MC and bind off center 13 (15, 15, 17) sts, k to end.
Dec row 1 (WS) With first ball of yarn, p to last 3 sts, p2tog tbl, p1; with 2nd ball of yarn, p1, p2tog, p to end.
Dec row 2 (RS) With first ball of yarn, k to last 3 sts, k2tog, k1; with 2nd ball of yarn, k1, ssk, k to end. Rep last 2 rows once more, then dec row 1 once. Purl next row. Rep dec row 2 on next row, then every other row 3 times more. Work even on 9 (11, 13, 14) sts each side until piece measures same length as back to shoulder, end with a WS row. Bind off each side for shoulders.

FINISHING
Block pieces to measurements. Sew right shoulder seam.

Neckband
With RS facing and MC, pick up and k 91 (95, 95, 99) sts evenly spaced along neck edge. Work in seed st for 3 (3, 5, 5) rows. Bind off loosely in seed st. Sew left shoulder and neckband seam.

Armbands
With RS facing and MC, pick up and k 69 (75, 83, 89) sts evenly spaced along armhole edge. Work in seed st for 3 (3, 5, 5) rows. Bind off loosely in seed st. Sew side seams. ∎

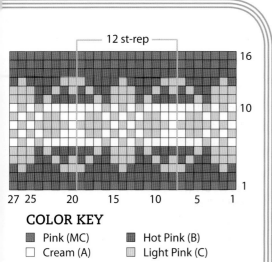

12 st-rep

16

10

1

27 25   20   15   10   5   1

COLOR KEY

- ■ Pink (MC)
- □ Cream (A)
- ■ Hot Pink (B)
- ▨ Light Pink (C)

1½ (2, 2¼, 2½)"

5½ (6, 6, 6¼)"

¾"

3"

5¼ (5¼, 5¾, 6¼)"

FRONT & BACK

18½ (20, 21½, 23)"

16 (17, 18, 19)"

17 (18, 20, 22)"

12½ (13½, 14½, 15½)"

TANK dress

SIZES
Sized for Child 2 (4, 6, 8, 10, 12). Shown in size 6.

MEASUREMENTS
Chest 22 (23½, 25½, 27½, 29½, 31)"/56 (58, 65, 70, 75, 78.5)cm
Length 20 (22, 24, 26½, 29½, 31)"/51 (56, 61, 67.5, 75, 79)cm

GAUGE
17 sts and 19 rows to 4"/10cm over k1, p1 rib using size 10 (6mm) needles.
Take time to check your gauge.

3-NEEDLE BIND-OFF
1 Hold right sides of pieces together on two needles. Insert third needle knitwise into first st of each needle, and wrap yarn knitwise.
2 Knit these two sts together, and slip them off the needles. *Knit the next two sts together in the same manner.
3 Slip first st on 3rd needle over 2nd st and off needle. Rep from * in step 2 across row until all sts are bound off.

MATERIALS

Yarn (5)
- 14oz/400g, 440yd, 410m (17½oz/500g, 550yd/510m; 17½oz/500g, 550yd/510m; 21oz/600g; 660yd/610m; 21oz/600g; 660yd/610m; 24½oz/700g, 770yd/710m) of any bulky weight cotton yarn in yellow

Needles
- One pair size 10 (6mm) needles *or size to obtain gauge*

Notion
- Stitch holders

BACK
With size 10 (6mm) needles, cast on 67 (73, 79, 85, 91, 97) sts. Work in seed st as foll:
Row 1 (RS) K1, *p1, k1; rep from * to end.
Row 2 K the purl sts and p the knit sts.
Rep row 2 for seed st until piece measures 11½ (12½, 13½, 14, 15½, 16)"/29 (32, 34, 35.5, 39.5, 40.5)cm from beg, end with a WS row.
Next (dec) row (RS) K1, *k2tog, k1; rep from * to end—45 (49, 53, 57, 61, 65) sts.
Row 1 (WS) K1, [k1, p1] 9 (10, 11, 12, 13, 14) times, k7, [p1, k1] 9 (10, 11, 12, 13, 14) times, k1. **Row 2** K1, [p1, k1] 9 (10, 11, 12, 13, 14) times, k7, [k1, p1] 9 (10, 11, 12, 13, 14) times, k1.
Rep the last 2 rows until piece measures 15 (16½, 18, 20½, 23, 24)"/38 (42, 45.5, 52, 58.5, 61)cm from beg, end with a WS row.

Armhole shaping
Bind off 2 (2, 2, 3, 3, 3) sts at beg of next 2 rows.
Next row (RS) K1, k2tog, work in pat to last 3 sts, SKP, k1.
Next row K1, work to last st, k1.
Rep the last 2 rows 2 (2, 2, 2, 3, 3) times more—35 (39, 43, 45, 47, 51) sts.
Work even until armhole measures 3¼ (3¾, 4¼, 4¼, 4¾, 5)"/8 (9.5, 11, 11.5, 12, 12.5)cm, end with a RS row.

Neck shaping
Next row (WS) Work 12 (13, 14, 15, 15, 17) sts, join a 2nd ball of yarn and bind off center 11 (13, 15, 15, 17, 17) sts, work to end. Working both sides at once, dec 1 st at each neck edge every row 5 times—7 (8, 9, 10, 10, 12) sts.
Work even until armhole measures 5 (5½, 6, 6, 6½, 7)"/13 (14, 15, 15, 16.5, 18)cm, end with a WS row. Leave rem sts each side for shoulder on holder.

FRONT
Work same as for back until armhole measures 1¼ (1¾, 2, 2, 2½, 3)"/3 (4.5, 5, 5.5, 6.5, 7.5)cm, end with a RS row.

Neck shaping
Next row (WS) Work 13 (15, 16, 17, 17, 19) sts, join a 2nd ball of yarn and bind off center 9 (9, 11, 11, 13, 13) sts, work to end. Working both sides at once, dec 1 st at each neck edge every row 4 times, then every other row 2 (3, 3, 3, 3, 3) times—7 (8, 9, 10, 10, 12) sts.
Work even until armhole measures same as back. Leave rem sts each side for shoulder on holder.

FINISHING
Join shoulder seams with 3-needle bind-off. Sew side seams. ■

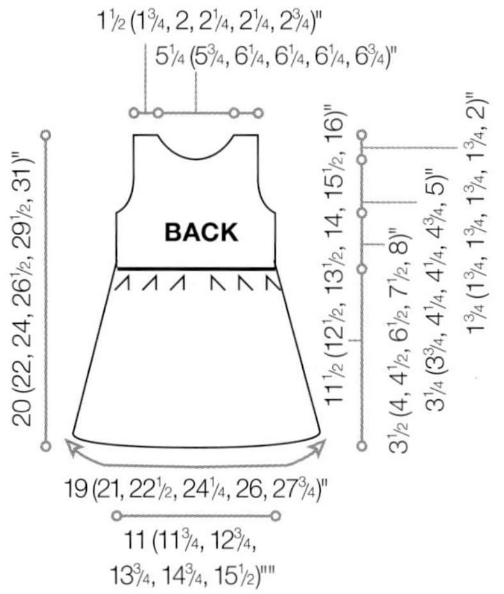
1½ (1¾, 2, 2¼, 2¼, 2¾)"
5¼ (5¾, 6¼, 6¼, 6¼, 6¾)"
BACK
20 (22, 24, 26½, 29½, 31)"
11½ (12½, 13½, 14, 15½, 16)"
3½ (4, 4½, 6½, 7½, 8)"
3¼ (3¾, 4¼, 4¼, 4¾, 5)"
1¾ (1¾, 1¾, 1¾, 1¾, 2)"
19 (21, 22½, 24¼, 26, 27¾)"
11 (11¾, 12¾, 13¾, 14¾, 15½)"

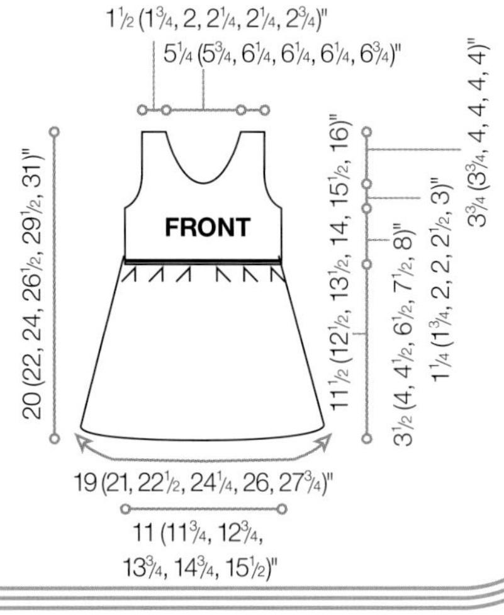
1½ (1¾, 2, 2¼, 2¼, 2¾)"
5¼ (5¾, 6¼, 6¼, 6¼, 6¾)"
FRONT
20 (22, 24, 26½, 29½, 31)"
11½ (12½, 13½, 14, 15½, 16)"
3½ (4, 4½, 6½, 7½, 8)"
1¼ (1¾, 2, 2, 2½, 3)"
3¾ (3¾, 4, 4, 4, 4)"
19 (21, 22½, 24¼, 26, 27¾)"
11 (11¾, 12¾, 13¾, 14¾, 15½)"

MULTI-ZIPPER cardigan

SIZES
Sizes for Child's 4, 6, 8, 10. Shown in size 4.

MEASUREMENTS
Chest (closed) 29 (31, 33, 35)"/73.5 (78.5, 84, 89)cm
Length 15 (17, 19, 20)"/38 (43, 48, 51)cm
Upper arm 9½ (10, 11, 11½)"/24 (25.5, 28, 29)cm

GAUGE
18 sts and 24 rows to 4"/10cm over St st using larger needles. *Take time to check your gauge.*

K1, P1, RIB
(over an odd number of sts)
Row 1 *K1, p1; rep from *, end k1.
Row 2 K the knit sts, and p the purl sts.
Rep row 2 for k1, p1 rib.

BACK
With smaller needles and MC, cast on 65 (69, 73, 77) sts. Work in k1, p1 rib for 2"/5cm, dec 1 (1, 1, 0) st on last row—64 (68, 72, 77) sts.
Change to larger needles and work in St st (k on RS, p on WS) until piece measures 9½ (11, 12½, 13)"/24 (28, 31.5, 33)cm from beg.

Shape armhole
Bind off 3 (4, 4, 5) sts at beg of next 2 rows, 2 (2, 3, 3) sts at beg of next 2 rows, dec 1 st each side every other row 4 (4, 4, 5) times—46 (48, 50, 51) sts. Work even until armhole measures 5½ (6, 6½, 7)"/14 (15, 16.5, 17.5)cm. Bind off all sts.

LEFT FRONT
With smaller needles and MC, cast on 33 (35, 37, 39) sts. Work in k1, p1 rib for 2"/5cm, dec 1 st on last row—32 (34,

36, 38) sts. Change to larger needles and work in St st until piece measures 4 (4½, 5, 5)"/10 (11.5, 12.5, 12.5)cm from beg, end with a WS row.
Zipper opening row (RS) K5 (6, 8, 9), bring yarn to front, slip next st purlwise. Place yarn at back and leave it there. *Slip next st from LH needle, pass the first slipped st over it; rep from * 17 times more (not moving the yarn). Slip the last bound-off st to LH needle and turn work. Cast on 19 sts (using the cable cast-on method) as foll: *with yarn at back of work, insert RH needle between the first and 2nd sts on LH needle and draw up a loop, place the loop on LH needle; rep from * 18 times more, turn work. Sl first st with yarn at back from LH needle and pass extra cast-on st over it, k to end of row. Cont in St st until piece measures 8 (9, 10,

MATERIALS
Yarn [4]
- 10½oz/300g, 660yd/600m (14oz/400g, 880yd/800m; 17½oz/500g, 1090yd/1000; 17½oz/500g, 1090yd/1000) of any worsted weight wool yarn in light purple (MC)
- 3½oz/100g, 220yd/200m in pale green (CC)

Needles
- One pair each sizes 6 and 8 (4 and 5mm) needles *or sizes to obtain guage*

Notions
- One separating zipper, 14 (16, 18, 18)"/30 (35, 45, 45)cm from Coats & Clark, F23 Style, #256 natural
- 4 all purpose zippers, 4"/10cm from Coats & Clark, F72 style, 2 each in #4 blue and #30 light pink
- Sewing needle, thread, and straight pins

10½)"/20.5 (23, 25.5, 26.5)cm from beg, end with a WS row.
Work zipper opening row. Cont in St st until piece measures 9½ (11, 12½, 13)"/24 (28, 31.5, 33)cm from beg. Shape armhole at side edge as for back on RS rows—23 (24, 25, 25) sts. Work even until armhole measures 3½ (4, 4½, 4)"/9 (10, 11.5, 10)cm, end with a RS row.

Shape neck
Next row (WS) Bind off 4 (5, 5, 5) sts (neck edge), work to end. Cont to bind off 2 sts from neck edge once, then dec 1 st every other row 3 times. Work even on rem 14 (14, 15, 15) sts until same length as back. Bind off sts for shoulder.

RIGHT FRONT
Work to correspond to left front, reversing all shaping by working armhole shaping on WS rows and neck shaping on RS rows, and working zipper opening row as foll:
Next row (RS) K9 (10, 10, 11), work bind off and cast on as for left front, k to end of row.

Pocket linings (make 4)
With CC, cast on 20 sts. Work in St st for 3½"/9cm. Bind off.

SLEEVES
With smaller needles and MC, cast on 29 (31, 31, 33) sts. Work in k1, p1 rib for 2"/5cm. Change to larger needles and work in St st, inc 1 st each side every 6th row 7 (7, 9, 9) times—43 (45, 49, 51) sts.
Work even until piece measures 11 (12, 13, 14)"/28 (30.5, 33, 35.5)cm from beg.

Shape cap
Bind off 3 (4, 4, 5) sts at beg of next 2 rows, 2 (2, 3, 3) sts at beg of next 2 rows, dec 1 st each side every other

row 2 (1, 1, 0) times, every 4th row 3 (4, 5, 6) times. Bind off 3 sts at beg of next 4 rows. Bind off rem 11 sts.

FINISHING
Block pieces to measurements. Sew 4"/10cm zippers into openings on fronts. Sew pocket linings to WS, with the bound-off edge of lining approx 1"/2.5cm above the pocket opening, and sew in place on all four sides. Sew shoulder seams. Set in sleeves. Sew side and sleeve seams.

Neckband
With RS facing, smaller needles and MC, pick up and k 55 (57, 57, 65) sts evenly around neck edge. Work in k1, p1 rib for 1"/2.5cm. Bind off in rib.

Right front band
With RS facing, smaller needles and CC, beg at lower edge and picking up sts 1 st in from edge, pick up and k 66 (75, 85, 85) sts evenly along right front edge, including side of neckband.
K 5 rows. Bind off all sts knitwise on RS.

Left front band
Work same as right front band, beg at top of neckband and ending at lower edge. Sew longer zipper to front garter st edge. Attach zipper pull if desired. ▨

Rose Callahan

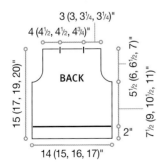

3 (3, 3¼, 3¼)"
4 (4½, 4½, 4¾)"
15 (17, 19, 20)"
BACK
5½ (6, 6½, 7)"
7½ (9, 10½, 11)"
2"
14 (15, 16, 17)"

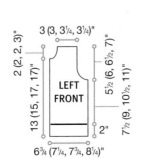

3 (3, 3¼, 3¼)"
2 (2, 2, 3)"
13 (15, 17, 17)"
LEFT FRONT
5½ (6, 6½, 7)"
7½ (9, 10½, 11)"
2"
6¾ (7¼, 7¾, 8¼)"

9½ (10, 11, 11½)"
4½, 5, 5½)"
SLEEVE
4 (4½, 5, 5½)"
9 (10, 11, 12)"
2"
6½ (7, 7, 7½)"

YELLOW EYELET dress

SIZES
Sized for Girl's 4, 6, 8. Shown in size 4.

MEASUREMENTS
Chest 24 (26½, 29)"/61 (67, 73.5)cm
Length 21 (23, 25)"/53.5 (58.5, 63.5)cm
Upper arm 10 (11, 12)"/25.5 (28, 30.5)cm

GAUGE
24 sts and 28 rows to 4"/10cm over St st using size 6 (4mm) needles.
Take time to check your gauge.

PATTERN STITCH
(multiple of 8 sts)
Row 1 and all WS rows Purl.
Row 2 (RS) Knit.
Row 4 K3, *yo, ssk, k6; rep from *, end last rep k3.
Row 6 K1, *k2tog, yo, k1, yo, ssk, k3; rep from *, end last rep k2.
Row 8 Rep row 4.
Row 10 Knit.
Row 12 K7, *yo, ssk, k6; rep from *, end k1.
Row 14 K5, *k2tog, yo, k1, yo, ssk, k3; rep from *, end k3.
Row 16 Rep row 12.
Rep rows 1–16 for pat st.

BACK BODICE
With straight needles, cast on 72 (80, 88) sts. Cont in pat st until piece measures 4 (4½, 5)"/10 (11.5, 12.5)cm from beg, end with a WS row.

Shape armholes
Bind off 4 (4, 5) sts at beg of next 2 rows. Dec 1 st each side on next row, then every other row 3 (4, 4) times more—56 (62, 68) sts. Work even until armhole measures 5 (5½, 6)"/12.5 (14, 15)cm, end with a WS row.

MATERIALS
Yarn (3)
- 10½oz/300g, 890yd/820m (14oz/400g, 1190yd/1090m; 15¾oz/450g, 1340yd/1230m) of any DK weight wool and cotton blend yarn in light yellow

Needles
- One pair size 6 (4mm) needles *or size to obtain gauge*
- One set (5) size 6 (4mm) double-pointed needles (dpns)
- Sizes 6 and 7 (4 and 4.5mm) circular needles, 24"/60cm long

Notions
- Size F/5 (3.75mm) crochet hook
- Stitch marker
- 2 (2¼, 2½)yd/2 (2.25, 2.5)m of 1½"/38mm wide ribbon

Shape shoulders
Bind off 4 (5, 5) sts at beg of next 4 rows, then 4 (4, 6) sts at beg of next 2 rows. Bind off rem 32 (34, 36) sts for back neck.

FRONT BODICE
Work as for back bodice until armhole measures 3½ (4, 4½)"/9 (10, 11.5)cm, end with a WS row—56 (62, 68) sts.

Shape neck
Next row (RS) Work across first 18 (20, 22) sts, join a 2nd ball of yarn and bind off center 20 (22, 24) sts, work to end. Working both sides at once, work next row even. Dec 1 st from each neck edge on next row, then every other row 5 times more. Work even on 12 (14, 16) sts each side until piece measures same length as back to shoulder, end with a WS row. Shape shoulders as for back.

SLEEVES
With straight needles, cast on 52 (56, 60) sts. Cont in St st for 1"/2.5cm, end with a WS row.
Next (picot) row (RS) K1, *k2tog, yo; rep from *, end k1. Purl next row. Cont in St st until piece measures 3 (2½, 2)"/7.5 (6.5, 5)cm from beg, end with a WS row. Inc 1 st each side on next row, then every 4th row 3 (4, 5) times more—60 (66, 72) sts. Work even until piece measures 5"/12.5cm from beg, end with a WS row.

Shape cap
Bind off 4 (4, 5) sts at beg of next 2 rows—52 (58, 62) sts. Work even until cap measures 2½ (3, 3½)"/6.5 (7.5, 9) cm, end with a WS row. Dec 1 st each side on next row, then every other row 3 times more, end with a WS row—44 (50, 54) sts.
Next (dec) row (RS) K2tog across—22 (25, 27) sts.
Next (dec) row P2 (4, 2), *p2tog, p3; rep from * across 3 (3, 4) times more, p0 (1, 0). Bind off rem 18 (21, 22) sts.

FINISHING
Block pieces to measurement. Sew shoulder seams. Set in sleeves. Sew side and sleeve seams. Fold bottom edge of each sleeve to WS along picot row and hem in place.

Skirt
With RS facing, smaller circular needle and beg at left side seam, pick up and k 1 st in each st around—144 (160, 176) sts. Join and pm for beg of rnd. K next rnd.
Next (inc) rnd K in front and back of each st around—288 (320, 352) sts. Work even in St st for 3"/7.5cm. Change to larger circular needle. Cont

in St st until skirt measures 10½ (11½, 12½)"/26.5 (29, 31.5)cm.

Next (picot) rnd *K2tog, yo; rep from * around. Work even for 1"/2.5cm. Bind off. Fold bottom edge skirt to WS along picot rnd and hem in place.

Neckband

With RS facing, dpns and beg at left shoulder seam, pick up and k 86 (90, 94) sts evenly spaced around neck edge, dividing sts evenly between 4 dpn. Join and pm for beg of rnds. Work around in k1, p1 rib for ¾"/2cm. Bind off loosely in rib.

Belt loops (make 2)

With crochet hook, make a chain 1¾"/4.5cm long. Fasten off. Sew each belt loop to side seams, just above beg of skirt. Thread ribbon through loops and tie at back. ◼

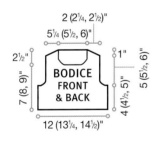

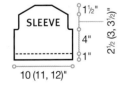

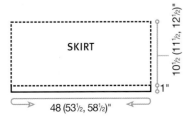

Rose Callahan

PEPLUM tunic

SIZES
Sized for Child 2 (4, 6, 8, 10, 12). Shown in size 6.

MEASUREMENTS
Chest 22 (23½, 25½, 27½, 29½, 31)"/56 (58, 65, 70, 75, 78.5)cm
Length 16 (17½, 19, 21, 23, 24½)"/40.5 (44.5, 48, 53.5, 58.5, 62)cm

GAUGE
17 sts and 19 rows to 4"/10cm over k1, p1 rib using size 10 (6mm) needles.
Take time to check your gauge.

3-NEEDLE BIND-OFF
1 Hold right sides of pieces together on two needles. Insert third needle knitwise into first st of each needle, and wrap yarn knitwise.
2 Knit these two sts together, and slip them off the needles. *Knit the next two sts together in the same manner.
3 Slip first st on 3rd needle over 2nd st and off needle. Rep from * in step 2 across row until all sts are bound off.

BACK
Skirt
With size 10 (6mm) needles, cast on 67 (73, 79, 85, 91, 97) sts. Work in seed st as foll:
Row 1 (RS) K1, *p1, k1; rep from * to end.
Row 2 K the purl sts and p the knit sts
Rep row 2 for seed st until piece measures 3"/7cm from beg, end with a WS row.

Bodice
Next (dec) row (RS) K1, *k2tog, k1; rep from * to end—45 (49, 53, 57, 61, 65) sts.
Row 1 (WS) K1, [k1, p1] 9 (10, 11, 12, 13, 14) times, k7, [p1, k1] 9 (10, 11, 12, 13, 14) times, k1.

MATERIALS
Yarn (5)
- 10½oz/300g, 330yd/310m (10½oz/300g, 330yd/310m; 10½oz/300g, 330yd/310m; 14oz/400g, 440yd/410m; 14oz/400g, 440yd/410m; 17½oz/500g; 550yd/500m) in any bulky weight cotton yarn in light pink

Needles
- One pair size 10 (6mm) needles
  or size to obtain gauge

Notions
- Stitch holders

Row 2 K1, [p1, k1] 9 (10, 11, 12, 13, 14) times, k7, [k1, p1] 9 (10, 11, 12, 13, 14) times, k1.
Rep the last 2 rows until piece measures 11 (12, 13, 15, 16½, 17½)"/28 (30.5, 33, 38, 42, 44.5)cm from beg, end with a WS row.

Armhole shaping
Bind off 2 (2, 2, 3, 3, 3) sts at beg of next 2 rows.
Next row (RS) K1, k2tog, work in pat to last 3 sts, SKP, k1.
Next row K1, work to last st, k1. Rep last 2 rows 2 (2, 2, 2, 3, 3) times more—35 (39, 43, 45, 47, 51) sts.
Work even until armhole measures 3¼ (3¾, 4¼, 4¼, 4¾, 5)"/8 (9.5, 11, 11.5, 12, 12.5)cm, end with a RS row.

Neck shaping
Next row (WS) Work in pat over 12 (13, 14, 15, 15, 17) sts, join a 2nd ball of yarn and bind off center 11 (13, 15, 15, 17, 17) sts, work to end. Working both sides at once, dec 1 st at each neck edge every row 5 times—7 (8, 9, 10, 10, 12) sts. Work even until armhole measures 5 (5½, 6, 6, 6½, 7)"/13 (14, 15, 15, 16.5, 18)cm, end with a WS row. Leave rem sts each side for shoulder on holder.

FRONT
Work same as for back until armhole measures 1¼ (1¾, 2, 2, 2½, 3)"/3 (4.5, 5, 5.5, 6.5, 7.5)cm, end with a RS row.

Neck shaping
Next row (WS) Work 13 (15, 16, 17, 17, 19) sts, join a 2nd ball of yarn and bind off center 9 (9, 11, 11, 13, 13) sts, work to end. Working both sides at once, dec 1 st at each neck edge every row 4 times, then every other row 2 (3, 3, 3, 3, 3) times—7 (8, 9, 10, 10, 12) sts. Work even until armhole measures same as back. Leave rem sts each side for shoulder on holder.

FINISHING
Join shoulder seams with 3-needle bind-off. Sew side seams. ▉

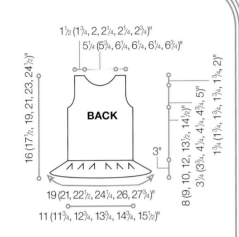

1½ (1¾, 2, 2¼, 2¼, 2¾)"

5¼ (5¾, 6¼, 6¼, 6¼, 6¾)"

16 (17½, 19, 21, 23, 24½)"

BACK

3"

1¾ (1¾, 1¾, 1¾, 1¾, 2)"

3¼ (3¾, 4¼, 4¼, 4¾, 5)"

8 (9, 10, 12, 13½, 14½)"

19 (21, 22½, 24¼, 26, 27¾)"

11 (11¾, 12¾, 13¾, 14¾, 15½)"

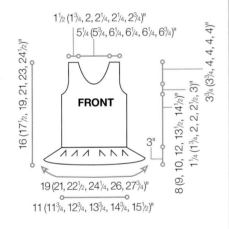

1½ (1¾, 2, 2¼, 2¼, 2¾)"

5¼ (5¾, 6¼, 6¼, 6¼, 6¾)"

16 (17½, 19, 21, 23, 24½)"

FRONT

3"

1¼ (1¾, 2, 2, 2½, 3)"

3¾ (3¾, 4, 4, 4, 4)"

8 (9, 10, 12, 13½, 14½)"

19 (21, 22½, 24¼, 26, 27¾)"

11 (11¾, 12¾, 13¾, 14¾, 15½)"

PICOT TRIM
dress

SIZES
Sized for Child's 2, 4, 6, 8, 10. Shown in size 4.

MEASUREMENTS
Chest 22 (24, 26, 27½, 29½)"/56 (61, 66, 70, 75)cm
Length 19 (20½, 22½, 25½, 28½)"/48 (52, 57, 64.5, 72.5)cm

GAUGE
18 sts and 26 rows to 4"/10cm over St st using size 8 (5mm) needles.
Take time to check your gauge.

RUFFLE STITCH
Row 1 (RS) *K3, p3; rep from * to end.
Row 2 *P3, k3; rep from * to end.
Rep rows 1 and 2 for ruffle stitch.

BACK
With straight needles and MC, cast on 156 (168, 180, 192, 204) sts. Work in ruffle st for 12 rows, end with a WS row.
Next (dec) row (RS) *S2KP, sl 1 purlwise, p2tog, psso; rep from * to end—52 (56, 60, 64, 68) sts.
Beg with a purl (WS) row, cont in St st (k on RS, p on WS) until piece measures 8 (9, 10½, 13, 15½)"/20.5 (23, 26.5, 33, 39.5)cm from beg, end with a WS row.
Next row K1, k2tog, k to last 3 sts, ssk, k1—50 (54, 58, 62, 66) sts. Work even until piece measures 14 (15½, 17, 19½, 22)"/35.5 (39.5, 43, 49.5, 56)cm from beg, end with a WS row.

Shape armhole
Bind off 2 (3, 3, 4, 4) sts at beg of next 2 rows, 2 sts at beg of next 2 rows. Dec 1 st each side of every RS row 0 (0, 1, 1, 2) times—42 (44, 46, 48, 50) sts. Work even until armhole measures 2½ (2½, 3, 3½, 4)"/6.5 (6.5, 7.5, 9, 10)cm, end with a WS row.

Divide for back neck
Next row (RS) K20 (21, 22, 23, 24), join a 2nd ball of yarn and bind off center 2 sts, k to end.
Working both sides at once, cont until armhole measures 5 (5, 5½, 6, 6½)"/13 (13, 14, 15, 16.5)cm, end with a WS row.

Shape shoulder
Place 10 (11, 11, 12, 12) sts from each shoulder edge on holder, bind off rem 10 (10, 11, 11, 12) sts for back neck.

FRONT
Work same as for back until armhole measures 3½ (3½, 4, 4, 4½)"/9 (9, 10, 10, 11.5)cm, end with a RS row—42 (44, 46, 48, 50) sts.

Shape neck
Next row (WS) K16 (17, 17, 18, 18), join a 2nd ball of yarn and bind off center 10 (10, 12, 12, 14) sts, work to end. Working both sides at once with separate balls of yarn, bind off from each neck edge 3 sts once, then 2 sts once. Dec 1 st at each

MATERIALS
Yarn ④
• 14oz/200g, 360yd/330m (17½oz/250g, 450yd/420m; 21oz/300g, 540yd/500m; 24½oz/350g, 630yd/580m; 31½oz/450g, 810yd/750m) of any worsted weight cotton yarn in purple (MC)
• 1¾oz/50g, 90yd/90m in aqua (CC)

Needles
• One pair size 8 (5mm) needles *or size to obtain guage*
• One set of size 8 (5mm) double-pointed needles (dpns)

Notions
• One size H/8 (5mm) crochet hook
• Stitch holders
• One ⅝"/1.5cm button

neck edge on next RS row once—10 (11, 11, 12, 12) sts. Work even until armhole measures same as back. Leave rem sts each side for shoulder on holder.

Pocket (make 2)
With size 8 (5mm) needles and MC, cast on 10 sts. Inc 1 st each side of next row, then every other row twice more—16 sts. Work even until piece measures 3"/7.5cm from beg, end with a WS row. Break MC and join CC. Work 2 rows more in St st.
Next (picot) row (RS) K1, *k2tog, yo; rep from * to last st, k1.
Work 2 rows St st, end with a RS row. Bind off all sts purlwise. Fold hem to WS at picot row and slip st in place.

FINISHING
Shoulder seams
Note Seam will be visible on RS of garment.
Join shoulders using 3-needle bind-off as foll: With wrong sides facing tog, and front of garment facing you, place sts of back and front left shoulders on 2 dpns. With a 3rd dpn and MC, k first stitch from front needle tog with first stitch from back needle, *k next stitch from front and back needles tog, slip first st over 2nd st to bind off; rep from * until all sts from needles are bound off.

Neckband
With RS facing, straight needles and CC, pick up and k 54 (54, 58, 62, 64) sts evenly around neck edge. P 1 row.
Next (picot) row K1, *k2tog, yo; rep from * to last st, k1.
Work 2 rows St st, end with a RS row. Bind off all sts purlwise. Fold hem to WS at picot row and slip st in place.

Armhole edging
With RS facing, straight needles and CC, pick up and k 48 (48, 52, 58, 62) sts evenly around armhole edge. Purl 1 row.

Next (picot) row K1, *k2tog, yo; rep from
* to last st, k1.
Work 2 rows St st, end with a RS row.
Bind off all sts purlwise. Sew side and
armhole edging seam. Fold hem to WS at
picot row on armhole edging and slip st
in place.

Button loop
With crochet hook and RS facing, join MC
with a slip st to top left back opening at
neck edge. Ch 6 and join with a slip st to
first ch. Fasten off.
Sew pockets to front as desired. Sew
button opposite buttonloop. ◼

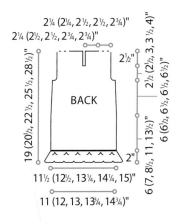

2¼ (2¼, 2½, 2½, 2¾)"
2¼ (2½, 2½, 2¾, 2¾)"

2½"

2½ (2½, 3, 3½, 4)"

BACK

19 (20½, 22½, 25½, 28½)"

6 (6½, 6½, 6½, 6½)"

2"

11½ (12½, 13¼, 14¼, 15)"

11 (12, 13, 13¾, 14¾)"

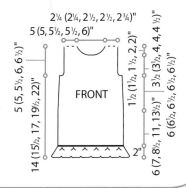

2¼ (2¼, 2½, 2½, 2¾)"
5 (5, 5½, 5½, 6)"

5 (5, 5½, 6, 6½)"

1½ (1½, 1½, 2, 2)"

3½ (3½, 4, 4, 4½)"

FRONT

14 (15½, 17, 19½, 22)"

6 (6½, 6½, 6½, 6½)"

2"

CABLED dress

SIZES
Sized for Child's 4, 6, 8, 10. Shown in size 6.

MEASUREMENTS
Chest 24 (26, 28, 30)"/61 (66, 71, 76)cm
Length 21 (22½, 24, 25½)"/53.5 (57, 61, 64.5)cm

GAUGE
16 sts and 22 rows to 4"/10cm over St st using size 9 (5.5mm) needles.
Take time to check your gauge.

STITCH GLOSSARY
4-st RC Sl 2 sts to cn, hold to *back*, k2, k2 from cn.
4-st LC Sl 2 sts to cn, hold to *front*, k2, k2 from cn.
8-st RC Sl 4 sts to cn, hold to *back*, k4, k4 from cn.
8-st LC Sl 4 sts to cn, hold to *front*, k4, k4 from cn.

K2, P2 RIB
(multiple of 4 sts plus 2)
Row 1 (RS) K2, *p2, k2; rep from * to end.
Row 2 P2, *k2, p2; rep from * to end.
Rep rows 1 and 2 for k2, p2 rib.

CABLE PATTERN 1
(over 8 sts)
Row 1 (RS) K8.
Rows 2, 4 and 6 P8.
Row 3 4-st RC, 4-st LC.
Rows 5 and 7 K8.
Row 8 P8.
Rep rows 1–8 for cable pat 1.

CABLE PATTERN 2
(over 16 sts)
Row 1 (RS) K16.
Rows 2, 4 and 6 P16.
Row 3 8-st RC, 8-st LC.
Rows 5 and 7 K16.

MATERIALS
Yarn 4
• 10½oz/300g, 470yd/430m (10½oz/300g, 470yd/430m; 14oz/400g, 620yd/570m; 14oz/400g, 620yd/570m) of any worsted weight wool yarn in cream

Needles
• One pair size 9 (5.5mm) needles *or size to obtain guage*
• Size 9 (5.5mm) circular needle, 16"/41cm long

Notions
• Cable needle (cn)
• Stitch markers

Row 8 P16.
Rep rows 1–8 for cable pat II.

BACK
Cast on 62 (66, 70, 74) sts. Work in k2, p2 rib for 6 rows. Cont in St st and work even for 8 (4, 2, 4) rows.

Shape sides
Dec row (RS) K1, ssk, k to last 3 sts, k2tog, k1. Rep dec row every 10th (12th, 14th, 14th) row 6 times more—48 (52, 56, 60) sts. Work even until piece measures 15 (16, 17, 18)"/38 (40.5, 43, 45.5)cm from beg, end with a WS row.

Shape armholes
Bind off 3 sts at beg of next 2 rows.
Dec row (RS) K1, ssk, k to last 3 sts, k2tog, k1. Work next row even. Rep last 2 rows twice more—36 (40, 44, 48) sts. Work even until armhole measures 1½ (2, 2½, 3)"/4 (5, 6.5, 7.5)cm, end with a WS row.

Shape neck
Next row (RS) Work across first 13 (14, 16, 17) sts, join a 2nd ball of yarn and bind off center 10 (12, 12, 14) sts, work

to end. Working both sides at once, work next row even. Dec 1 st from each neck edge on next row, then every other row 3 times more. Work even on 9 (10, 12, 13) sts each side until armhole measures 6 (6½, 7, 7½)"/15 (16.5, 18, 19)cm, end with a WS row. Bind off each side for shoulders.

FRONT
Cast on 74 (78, 82, 86) sts. Work in k2, p2 rib for 6 rows.

Beg cable pats
Note Cable pat may be worked using written or charted instructions.
Row 1 (RS) K14 (15, 16, 17), pm, work cable pat 1 or chart 1 over next 8 sts, pm, k7 (8, 9, 10), pm, work cable pat 2 or chart 2 over center 16 sts, pm, k7 (8, 9, 10), pm, work cable pat 1 or chart 1 over next 8 sts, pm, k4 (15, 16, 17). Keeping sts each side of cable pats in St st, cont to work cable pats through row 8, then rep rows 1–8 to end, AT THE SAME TIME, when 8 (4, 2, 4) rows have been completed, end with a WS row.

Shape sides
Work as for back—60 (64, 68, 72) sts. Work even until piece measures same length as back to underarm, end with a WS row.

Shape armholes
Work as for back—48 (52, 56, 60) sts. Work even until armhole measures 1½ (2, 2½, 3)"/4 (5, 6.5, 7.5)cm, end with a WS row.

Shape neck
Next row (RS) Work across first 16 (17, 19, 20) sts, join a 2nd ball of yarn and bind off center 16 (18, 18, 20) sts, work to end. Working both sides at once, work next row even. Dec 1 st from each neck edge on next row, then every other row 4

times more. Work even on 11 (12, 14, 15) sts each side until armhole measures 6 (6½, 7, 7½)"/15 (16.5, 18, 19)cm, end with a WS row. Bind off each side for shoulders.

FINISHING
Block pieces to measurements. Sew shoulder seams.

Neckband
With RS facing and circular needle, beg at left shoulder seam and pick up and k 92 (96, 96, 100) sts evenly spaced around entire neck edge. Join and pm for beg of rnds. Work around in k2, p2 rib for 5 (5, 6, 6) rnds. Bind off in rib.

Armbands
With RS facing and straight needles, pick up and k 54 (58, 62, 66) sts evenly spaced along armhole edge. Work in k2, p2 rib for 2 (2, 4, 4) rows. Bind off loosely in rib. Sew side seams. ■

Rose Callahan

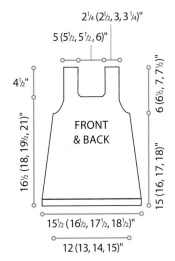

2¼ (2½, 3, 3¼)"

5 (5½, 5½, 6)"

4½"

FRONT & BACK

16½ (18, 19½, 21)"

6 (6½, 7, 7½)"

15 (16, 17, 18)"

15½ (16½, 17½, 18½)"

12 (13, 14, 15)"

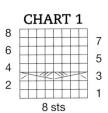

CHART 1

8
6
4
2

7
5
3
1

8 sts

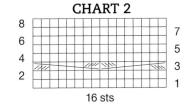

CHART 2

8
6
4
2

7
5
3
1

16 sts

STITCH KEY

☐ k on RS, p on WS

4-st RC

4-st LC

8-st RC

8-st LC

PULLOVER
purse and scarf

SIZES
Sized for girl's 8 (10, 12, 14). Shown in size 8.

MEASUREMENTS
Sleeveless pullover
Chest 27 (29, 31, 33)"/68.5 (73.5, 79, 84)cm
Length 15 (16, 17½, 18½)"/38 (40.5, 44.5, 47)cm

Scarf
Approx 5½ x 43½"/15 x 110.5cm

Purse
Approx 7½ x 6"/19 x 15cm

GAUGE
18 sts and 24 rows to 4"/10cm over St st using size 8 (5mm) needles.
Take time to check your gauge.

Sleeveless Pullover
BACK
With MC, cast on 60 (66, 70, 74) sts. Work in St st for 10 (10½, 11½, 12)"/25.5 (26.5, 29, 30.5)cm, end with a WS row.

Shape armholes
Bind off 3 (3, 4, 4) sts at beg of next 2 rows, then 1 st at each side on every other row 2 (3, 3, 4) times—50 (54, 56, 58) sts. Work even in until armhole measures 4½ (4¾, 5¼, 5¾)"/11 (12, 13, 14.5)cm, end with a WS row.

Shape neck and shoulders
Next row (RS) K15 (17, 17, 18), join a 2nd ball of yarn and bind off 20 (20, 22, 22) sts, work to end. Working both sides at once, bind off 4 sts at each neck edge once—11 (13, 13, 14) sts for

each shoulder. Work even until armhole measures 5 (5½, 6, 6½)"/12.5 (14, 15, 16.5)cm. Bind off.

FRONT
Work as for back until armhole measures 2¾ (3, 3½, 4)"/6.5 (7.5, 9, 10)cm, end with a WS row.

Shape neck
Next row (RS) K21 (23, 23, 24) sts, join a 2nd ball of yarn and bind off 8 (8, 10, 10) sts, k to end. Working both sides at once, bind off 3 sts at each neck edge twice, then 2 sts at each neck edge once, then 1 st at each neck edge on every other row twice—11 (13, 13, 14) sts for each shoulder. Work even until armhole measures same as back. Bind off.

FINISHING
Sew shoulder and side seams. With CC and crochet hook, work 1 rnd sc around neck, armhole and lower edges. (See stitch details on opposite page.)

MATERIALS
Yarn ④
- 12¼oz/350g, 960yd/880m (12¼oz/350g, 960yd/880m; 12¼oz/350g, 960yd/880m; 14oz/400g, 1090yd/1000m) of any worsted weight cotton and acrylic blend yarn in red (MC)
- 1¾oz/50g, 140yd/130m in white (CC)

Needles
- One pair size 8 (5mm) needles *or size to obtain gauge*
- One set (2) size 8 (5mm) double-pointed needles (dpns)
- Size G/6 (4mm) crochet hook

Scarf
With MC, cast on 24 sts. Work even in St st until piece measures 43½"/110.5 cm. Bind off.

FINISHING
With CC and crochet hook, work 1 rnd of sc around entire outside edge of scarf, join with sl st to first st. Fasten off.

Purse
With MC, cast on 34 sts. Work even in St st until piece measures 15½"/39cm. Bind off. Fold piece over, with RS out, so that 3½"/9cm overlaps the front to form a flap. Sew side seams. Fold up ¾"/2 cm of flap so that WS shows and pin in place. With CC and yarn needle, work cross stitches over 2 rows and 3 sts, working through both thicknesses of the flap. Work a vertical stitch over the point where the cross stitches intersect. (See stitch details on opposite page.)

Strap
With dpns, cast on 3 sts.
Row 1 K, do not turn. *Slide sts to opposite end of needle to work next row from RS, pulling yarn taut across back, and k3; rep from * until strap measures 47"/120 cm from beg. Bind off. Sew strap ends to purse. ∎

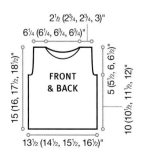

Seppo Saarentola/Moda

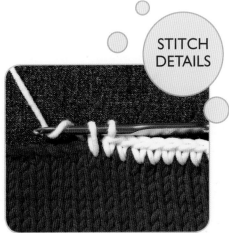

A row of single crochet in a contrasting color adds a tailored border to the outer edges of the vest and scarf.

For the purse-flap embroidery, make a cross-stitch with two ¾"/2cm stitches. Then, make a ¼"/6mm vertical stitch over the intersection of the cross-stitch.

TANK top

SIZES
Sized for Child 2 (4, 6, 8, 10, 12). Shown in size 6.

MEASUREMENTS
Chest 22 (23½, 25½, 27½, 29½, 31)"/56 (58, 65, 70, 75, 78.5)cm
Length 13 (14½, 16, 18, 20, 21½)"/33 (37, 40.5, 45.5, 51, 54.5)cm

GAUGE
17 sts and 19 rows to 4"/10cm over k1, p1 rib using size 10 (6mm) needles.
Take time to check your gauge.

3-NEEDLE BIND-OFF
1 Hold right sides of pieces together on two needles. Insert third needle knitwise into first st of each needle, and wrap yarn knitwise.
2 Knit these two sts together, and slip them off the needles. *Knit the next two sts together in the same manner.
3 Slip first st on 3rd needle over 2nd st and off needle. Rep from * in step 2 across row until all sts are bound off.

BACK
With size 10 (6mm) needles, cast on 45 (49, 53, 57, 61, 65) sts.
Row 1 (WS) K1, [k1, p1] 9 (10, 11, 12, 13, 14) times, k7, [p1, k1] 9 (10, 11, 12, 13, 14) times, k1.
Row 2 K1, [p1, k1] 9 (10, 11, 12, 13, 14) times, k7, [k1, p1] 9 (10, 11, 12, 13, 14) times, k1.
Rep the last 2 rows until piece measures 8 (9, 10, 12, 13½, 14½)"/20.5 (23, 25.5, 30.5, 34, 37)cm from beg, end with a WS row.

Armhole shaping
Bind off 2 (2, 2, 3, 3, 3) sts at beg of next 2 rows.

MATERIALS
Yarn 🧶5
• 7oz/200g, 220yd/210m (10½oz/300g, 330yd/310m; 10½oz/300g, 330yd/310m; 10½oz/300g, 330yd/310m; 14oz/400g, 440yd/410m; 14oz/400g, 440yd/410m) of any bulky weight cotton yarn in orange

Needles
• One pair size 10 (6mm) needles *or size to obtain gauge*

Notions
• Stitch holders

Next row (RS) K1, k2tog, work in pat to last 3 sts, SKP, k1.
Next row K1, work to last st, k1.
Rep the last 2 rows 2 (2, 2, 2, 3, 3) times more—35 (39, 43, 45, 47, 51) sts.
Work even until armhole measures 3¼ (3¾, 4¼, 4¼, 4¾, 5)"/8 (9.5, 11, 11.5, 12, 12.5)cm, end with a RS row.

Neck shaping
Next row (WS) Work 12 (13, 14, 15, 15, 17) sts, join a 2nd ball of yarn and bind off center 11 (13, 15, 15, 17, 17) sts, work to end. Working both sides at once, dec 1 st at each neck edge every row 5 times—7 (8, 9, 10, 10, 12) sts. Work even until armhole measures 5 (5½, 6, 6, 6½, 7)"/13 (14, 15, 15, 16.5, 18)cm, end with a WS row. Leave rem sts each side for shoulder on holder.

FRONT
Work same as for back until armhole measures 1¼ (1¾, 2, 2, 2½, 3)"/3 (4.5, 5, 5.5, 6.5, 7.5)cm, end with a RS row.

Neck shaping
Next row (WS) Work 13 (15, 16, 17, 17, 19) sts, join a 2nd ball of yarn and bind off center 9 (9, 11, 11, 13, 13) sts, work to end. Working both sides at once, dec 1 st at each neck edge every row 4 times, then every other row 2 (3, 3, 3, 3, 3) times—7 (8, 9, 10, 10, 12) sts. Work even until armhole measures same as back. Leave rem sts each side for shoulder on holder.

FINISHING
Join shoulder seams with 3-needle bind-off. Sew side seams. ▓

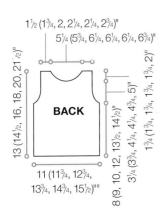

1½ (1¾, 2, 2¼, 2¼, 2¾)"
5¼ (5¾, 6¼, 6¼, 6¼, 6¾)"

13 (14½, 16, 18, 20, 21½)"

BACK

1¼ (1¾, 1¾, 1¾, 1¾, 2)"
3¼ (3¾, 4¼, 4¼, 4¾, 5)"

11 (11¾, 12¾, 13¾, 14¾, 15½)"

8 (9, 10, 12, 13½, 14½)"

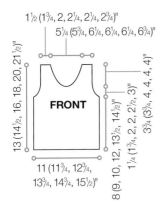

1½ (1¾, 2, 2¼, 2¼, 2¾)"
5¼ (5¾, 6¼, 6¼, 6¼, 6¾)"

13 (14½, 16, 18, 20, 21½)"

FRONT

1¼ (1¾, 2, 2, 2½, 3)"
3¾ (3¾, 4, 4, 4, 4)"

11 (11¾, 12¾, 13¾, 14¾, 15½)"

8 (9, 10, 12, 13½, 14½)"

Paul Amato for Lvarepresents.com

GIRL'S hoodie

SIZES
Sized for girl's 8 (10, 12, 14). Shown in size 8.

MEASUREMENTS
Chest 30 (32, 33½, 34½)"/76 (81.5, 85, 87.5)cm
Length 17 (18½, 19½, 21¾)"/43 (47, 49.5, 55)cm
Upper arm 12½ (12¾, 13¾, 14½)"/32 (32.5, 35, 37)cm

GAUGE
18 sts and 24 rows to 4"/10cm over St st using size 8 (5mm) needles.
Take time to check your gauge.

BACK
With MC, cast on 68 (72, 76, 78) sts. Work in k1, p1 rib for 2 rows.
Next row (RS) K34 (36, 38, 39); p34 (36, 38, 39).

MATERIALS
Yarn (4)
• 17½oz/500g, 1360yd/1250m (17½oz/500g, 1360yd/1250m; 19¼oz/550g, 1500yd/1380m; 21oz/600g, 1640yd/1500m) of any worsted weight cotton and acrylic blend yarn in white (MC)
• 1¾oz/50g, 140yd/130m in red (CC)

Needles
• One pair size 8 (5mm) needles *or size to obtain gauge*

Notions
• Yarn needle

Next row (WS) K34 (36, 38, 39); p34 (36, 38, 39). Cont in St st (k on RS, p on WS) on right half of piece and rev St st (p on RS, k on WS) on left half as established until piece measures 8¼ (9, 10, 10½)"/21 (23, 25, 27)cm from beg, end with a WS row.
Next row (RS) Switch position of St st and rev St st, working right half in rev St st and left half in St st. Cont in this way until piece measures 10 (11, 11¾, 13½)"/25 (28, 30, 34)cm from beg, end with a WS row.

Shape armholes
Bind off 2 sts at beg of next 2 rows.
Next (dec) row (RS) P2, p2tog, work in pat as established to last 4 sts, k2tog, k2.
Next row (WS) Work in pat as established. Rep last 2 rows 3 times more—56 (60, 64, 66) sts.
Work even until armhole measures 6¼ (6¾ 7, 7½)"/16 (17, 18, 19)cm, end with a WS row.

Shape back neck
Next row (RS) P17 (19, 20, 21), join a 2nd ball of yarn and bind off 22 (22, 24, 24) sts, work to end in pat. Working both sides at once, bind off 3 sts at each neck

edge—14 (16, 17, 18) sts. Work even in pat until armhole measures 7 (7½, 7¾, 8¼)"/18 (19, 20, 21)cm. Bind off.

FRONT
Work as for back until armhole measures 4 (4¼, 4¾, 5¼)"/10 (11, 12, 13) cm from beg, end with a WS row.
Next row (RS) P22 (24, 25, 26), join a 2nd ball of yarn and bind off 12 (12, 14, 14) sts, k to end. Working both sides at once, bind off 3 sts at each neck edge once, 2 sts at each neck edge once, then dec 1 st at each neck edge every other row 3 times—14 (16, 17, 18) sts. Work even in pat until armhole measures same as back to shoulder. Bind off.

POCKET
With MC and RS facing, pick up and k 68 (72, 76, 78) sts along upper edge of ribbing on front, work in St st and rev St st to match front until pocket measures 2¼ (2¾, 3¼, 3½)"/6 (7, 8, 9)cm, end with a WS row.

Shape sides
Row 1 (RS) K2, SKP, work in pat to last 4 sts, p2tog, p2. Rep last row 15 times more, then rep row 1 on RS only (every other row) 4 times more—28 (32, 36, 38) sts. Match rem sts of pocket to front and graft pocket sts to front, or bind off rem sts and sew top edge of pocket to front.

LEFT SLEEVE
With MC, cast on 30 (32, 34, 36) sts. Work in k1, p1 rib for 2 rows. Work even in St st until piece measures 4"/10 cm from beg, end with a WS row. Inc 1 st each side on next row and then every 6th row 3 (6, 7, 8) times more; then every 4th row 9 (6, 6, 6) times more—56 (58, 62, 66) sts. Work even until sleeve measures 14½ (15½, 17, 18)"/37 (39, 43, 46)cm from beg.

GIRL'S hoodie

Shape cap
Bind off 2 sts at beg of next 2 rows. Dec 1 st each side on next row and then every other row 3 times more—44 (46, 50, 54) sts. Bind off.

RIGHT SLEEVE
Work as for left sleeve, but work in rev St st.

HOOD
Note Hood is worked from front edge to back of the neck.

With MC, cast on 94 (96, 96, 100) sts. Work in k1, p1 rib for 2 rows. Work even in St st until piece measures 3½"/9 cm from beg, end with a WS row. Dec 1 st at each side on next row and then every other row 5 times more—82 (84, 84, 88) sts. Work even until piece measures 8½ (8½, 9½, 9½)"/22 (22, 24, 24)cm from beg. Bind off.

FINISHING
Sew shoulder seams. Sew neck edge of hood to neck (see photo). Set in sleeves. Sew the first 2"/5cm of each sleeve seam with WS tog for turning of cuff. Sew rem sleeve seams and side seams. With yarn needle and CC, embroider a vertical and a horizontal line of running sts to demarcate the 4 different sections of knitting on the front and back, weaving under and over 2 rows vertically and under and over 1 st horizontally. With CC, embroider a line of running sts under and over 1 st along upper edge of rib on each sleeve end. With CC, make a 48"/120cm long twisted cord and weave it under and over 2 sts along front edge of the hood. (See below for details.) ▇

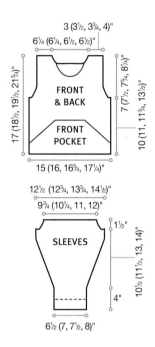

3 (3½, 3¾, 4)"
6¼ (6¼, 6½, 6½)"
17 (18½, 19½, 21¾)"
7 (7½, 7¾, 8¼)"
FRONT & BACK
FRONT POCKET
10 (11, 11¾, 13½)"
15 (16, 16¾, 17¼)"

12½ (12¾, 13¾, 14½)"
9¾ (10¼, 11, 12)"
1½"
SLEEVES
10½ (11½, 13, 14)"
4"
6½ (7, 7½, 8)"

EASY ACCENTS

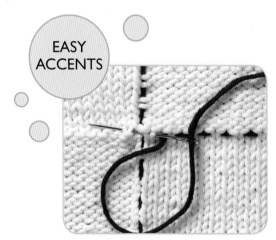

Embroider running stitch by weaving yarn under and over 2 knit rows vertically and 1 stitch horizontally.

Make 1½ yards/1.4m of twisted cord from red yarn and weave it under and over 2 stitches along the hood edge.

CHILD'S tank top

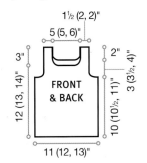

Rose Callahan

MATERIALS

Yarn
- 5¼oz/150g, 410yd/380m (5¼oz/150g, 410yd/380m; 7oz/200g, 550yd/510m) of any DK weight cotton yarn in blue

Needles
- One pair size 6 (4mm) needles *or size to obtain guage*

Notions
- Size G/6 (4mm) crochet hook

SIZES
Sized for child's 3, 5 and 7. Shown in size 3.

MEASUREMENTS
Chest 22 (24, 26)"/56 (61, 66)cm
Length 15 (16, 17)"/38 (40.5, 43)cm

GAUGE
16 sts and 32 rows to 4"/10cm over St st using size 6 (4mm) needles.
Take time to check your gauge.

STITCH GLOSSARY
SPP Slip 1, p1, psso.

SAND STITCH
(multiple of 4 sts)
Row 1 (RS) *K1, p1; rep from * to end of row.
Rows 2 and 4 Purl
Row 3 *P1, k1; rep from * to end of row.
Repeat rows 1–4 for sand st.

BACK
With size 6 (4mm) needles, cast on 66 (72, 78) sts. Work in sand st for 8 rows. Change to St st (k on RS, p on WS) and work until piece measures 5 (5½, 6)"/12.5 (14, 15)cm from beg. Work 8 rows in sand st. Change to St st and

work for 3½"/9cm more. Work 4 rows of sand st. Change to St st and work until piece measures 10 (10½, 11)"/25 (26.5, 28) cm from beg.

Shape armhole
Bind off 6 sts at beg of next 2 rows.
Next (dec) row (RS) K1, ssk, k to last 3 sts of row, k2tog, k1. Rep dec row every RS row two times more—48 (54, 60) sts. Work even in St st until piece measures 12 (13, 14)"/30.5 (33, 35.5)cm from beg.

Make eyelet heart
Next row K22 (25, 28), k2tog, yo, ssk, k to end of row—47 (53, 59) sts.
Next row Purl.
Next (RS) row K21 (24, 27), k2tog, yo, k1, yo, ssk, k to end of row. Cont in St st 3 rows more.

Shape neck
Next (RS) row K15 (18, 18), join second ball of yarn, bind off next 17 (17, 23) sts, k to end.
Next row Purl.
Dec row 1 (RS) K to 3 sts before neck edge, k2tog, k1, (left side of neck) K1, ssk, k to end of row.
Next row P to 3 sts before neck edge, p2tog, (right side of neck) p1, spp, p to end of row. Rep Dec row 1 every RS row 4 times more—9 (12, 12) sts each shoulder. Cont until piece measures 15 (16, 17)"/38 (40.5, 43)cm from beg. Bind off.

FRONT
Work same as for back until piece measures 12 (13,14)"/30.5 (33, 35.5)cm from beg.

Shape neck
Next (RS) row K15 (18, 18), join second ball of yarn, bind off next 18 (18, 24) sts, k to end.
Next row Purl.
Dec row 1 (RS) K to 3 sts before neck edge, k2tog, k1, (left side of neck) K1, ssk, k to end.
Next row P to 3 sts before neck edge, p2tog, (right side of neck) p1, spp, p to end of row. Rep dec row 1 every RS row 4 times more—9 (12, 12) sts each shoulder. Cont until piece measures 15 (16, 17)"/38 (40.5, 43)cm from beg. Bind off.

FINISHING
Sew shoulders and side seams. Crochet 1 rnd of sc around neck and sleeve openings. ∎

1½ (2, 2)"
5 (5, 6)"
3"
2"
3 (3½, 4)"
12 (13, 14)"
FRONT & BACK
10 (10½, 11)"
11 (12, 13)"

CARDIGAN

SIZES
Sized for Child's 4, 6, 8, 10. Shown in size 6.

MEASUREMENTS
Chest (buttoned) 23 (25, 28, 31)"/58.5 (63.5, 71, 78.5)cm
Length 13 (14, 15, 16)"/33 (35.5, 38, 40.5)cm
Upper arm 10 (10¾, 11½, 12½)"/25.5 (27.5, 29, 31.5)cm

GAUGE
20 sts and 26 rows to 4"/10cm over St st using size 7 (4.5mm) needles.
Take time to check your gauge.

STITCH GLOSSARY
6-st RC Sl 3 sts to cn, hold to *back*, k3, k3 from cn.
6-st LC Sl 3 sts to cn, hold to *front*, k3, k3 from cn.

K2, P2 RIB
(multiple of 4 sts plus 2)
Row 1 (RS) K2, *p2, k2; rep from * to end.
Row 2 P2, *k2, p2; rep from * to end.
Rep rows 1 and 2 for k2, p2 rib.

CABLE PATTERN
(over 12 sts)
Row 1 (RS) K12.
Rows 2, 4 and 6 P12.
Row 3 6-st RC, 6-st LC.
Rows 5 and 7 K12.
Row 8 P12.
Rep rows 1–8 for cable pat.

BACK
Cast on 58 (62, 70, 78) sts. Work in k2, p2 rib for 2"/5cm, end with a WS row. Cont in St st and work even until piece measures 7½ (8, 8½, 9)"/19 (20.5, 21.5, 23)cm from beg.

MATERIALS
Yarn 4
• 14oz/400g, 700yd/640m (14oz/400g, 700yd/640m; 17½oz/500g, 840yd/770m; 21oz/600g, 1010yd/930m) of any worsted weight wool yarn in variegated pink

Needles
• One pair size 7 (4.5mm) needles *or size to obtain guage*

Notions
• Cable needle (cn)
• Stitch markers
• Five 1"/25mm buttons

Shape armholes
Bind off 4 (4, 5, 5) sts at beg of next 2 rows. Dec 1 st each side on next row, then every other row 2 (2, 3, 4) times more—44 (48, 52, 58) sts. Work even until armhole measures 5½ (6, 6½, 7)"/14 (15, 16.5, 17.5)cm, end with a WS row. Bind off.

LEFT FRONT
Cast on 34 (34, 38, 42) sts. Work in k2, p2 rib for 2"/5cm, dec 2 (0, 0, 0) sts evenly spaced across last WS row—32 (34, 38, 42) sts.

Beg cable pat
Note Cable pat may be worked using written text above or using chart.
Row 1 (RS) K9 (10, 12, 14), pm, work cable pat over next 12 sts, pm, k11 (12, 14, 16).
Row 2 P to first marker, work cable pat to next marker, p to end. Keeping sts each side of cable pat in St st, cont in cable pat until row 8 is complete, then rep rows 1–8 to end, AT THE SAME TIME, when piece measures same length as back to underarm, end with a WS row.

Shape armhole
Bind off 4 (4, 5, 5) sts at beg of next row. Work next row even. Dec 1 st from armhole edge on next row, then every other row 2 (2, 3, 4) times more—25 (27, 29, 32) sts. Work even until armhole measures 2 (2½, 3, 3½)"/5 (6.5, 7.5, 9) cm, end with a RS row.

Shape neck
Next row (WS) Bind off 5 (5, 6, 7) sts, work to end. Dec 1 st from neck edge on next row, then every other row 3 (3, 4, 4) times more—16 (18, 18, 20) sts. Work even until piece measures same length as back to shoulder, end with a WS row. Bind off.

RIGHT FRONT
Cast on 34 (34, 38, 42) sts. Work in k2, p2 rib for 2"/5cm, dec 2 (0, 0, 0) sts evenly spaced across last WS row—32 (34, 38, 42) sts.

Beg cable pat
Row 1 (RS) K11 (12, 14, 16), pm, work cable pat over next 12 sts, pm, k9 (10, 12, 14).
Row 2 P to first marker, work cable pat to next marker, p to end. Cont as for left front, reversing all shaping.

SLEEVES
Cast on 38 (38, 42, 42) sts. Work in k2, p2 rib for 1¾"/4.5cm, end with a WS row. Cont in St st and work even for 2 rows. Inc 1 st each side on next row, then every 8th row 0 (7, 3, 9) times more, then every 10th row 5 (0, 4, 0) times—50 (54, 58, 62) sts. Work even until piece measures 11 (12, 13, 14)"/28 (30.5, 33, 35.5) cm from beg, end with a WS row.

Shape cap
Bind off 4 (4, 5, 5) sts at beg of next 2 rows. Dec 1 st each side on next row,

Buttonband
With RS facing, pick up and k 54 (58, 62, 70) sts evenly spaced along left front edge. Beg with row 2, work in k2, p2 rib for 9 rows. Bind off loosely in rib. Place markers for 5 buttons along buttonband, with the first ¾"/2cm from lower edge, the last 1½"/4cm below neck edge and the others evenly spaced between.

Buttonhole band
With RS facing, pick up and k 54 (58, 62, 70) sts evenly spaced along right front edge. Beg with row 2, work in k2, p2 rib for 3 rows.
Next (buttonhole) row (RS) *Work in rib to marker, bind off next 3 sts; rep from * 4 times more, work in rib to end.
Next row Work in rib, casting-on 3 sts over bound-off sts. Cont in k2, p2 rib for 4 rows more. Bind off loosely in rib. Set in sleeves. Sew side and sleeve seams. Sew on buttons. ■

then every other row 2 (2, 3, 4) times more, then every row 10 (12, 12, 12) times. Bind off 2 sts at beg of next 4 rows. Bind off rem 8 (8, 8, 10) sts.

FINISHING
Block pieces to measurements. Sew shoulder seams.

Neckband
With RS facing, pick up and k 66 (66, 72, 76) sts evenly spaced along entire neck edge. Beg with row 2, work in k2, p2 rib for 7 rows. Bind off in rib.

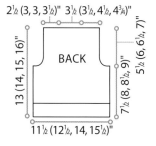

BACK

2½ (3, 3, 3½)" 3½ (3½, 4½, 4¾)"

13 (14, 15, 16)"

5½ (6, 6½, 7)"

7½ (8, 8½, 9)"

11½ (12½, 14, 15½)"

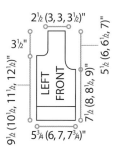

2½ (3, 3, 3½)"

3½"

LEFT FRONT

9½ (10½, 11½, 12½)"

5½ (6, 6½, 7)"

7½ (8, 8½, 9)"

5¾ (6, 7, 7¾)"

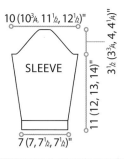

10 (10¾, 11½, 12½)"

SLEEVE

3½ (3¾, 4, 4¼)"

11 (12, 13, 14)"

7 (7, 7½, 7½)"

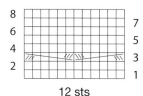

8
6
4
2

7
5
3
1

12 sts

STITCH KEY
☐ k on RS, p on WS

▨▨▨ 6-st RC

▨▨▨ 6-st LC